TITANIC &
HER SISTERS

A Postcard History

JANETTE & CAMPBELL MCCUTCHEON

AMBERLEY

A rare Russian postcard, posted in 1913, showing the *Titanic* hitting the iceberg. This is the only Russian-published card the authors have ever seen, and purchased a mere week before this book was heading to print. Two people from Russia were aboard *Titanic*. Husband and wife Sinai and Miriam Kantor sailed from Southampton on ticket 244367. Mrs Kantor survived and was rescued on boat 12, while her husband's body was recovered by the cable ship *Mackay-Bennett* as body 283.

First published 2014

Amberley Publishing
The Hill, Stroud
Gloucestershire, GL5 4EP

www.amberley-books.com

ISBN 978 1 84868 110 1 (print)
ebook ISBN 978 1 4456 3710 5 (ebook)

British Library Cataloguing in Publication Data.
A catalogue record for this book is available from the British Library.

Typeset in 11pt on 12pt Sabon LT Std.
Typesetting by Amberley Publishing.
Printed in the UK.

CONTENTS

Chapter One

A DINNER DATE WITH DESTINY

So the story goes, over dinner, the discussion came round to other shipping lines and the building of new ocean liners. Cunard's *Lusitania* had entered service, *Mauretania* was to follow soon afterwards and while White Star had its Big Four, it had no superliner to compete with the Cunard pair. Lord Pirrie, of Harland & Wolff, had invited J. Bruce Ismay, the Chairman of the White Star Line, and his wife to dine at his home, Downshire House, Belgrave Square, London. Both men drew plans for a trio of superliners, a full third larger than the Cunard liners, which were then the largest man-made objects in existence. Designed not to win the Blue Riband, but for comfort and elegance, the ships would have three funnels and four masts, with the first two being built on the new slipways that Pirrie was having constructed at his Belfast shipyard. Once one was complete, its slipway would be used to build the third ship. With three large vessels, White Star could operate a weekly service from Southampton to New York, both economically and profitably. The ships were to be the height of luxury, with every possible convenience on board, including large restaurants, Turkish Baths and a swimming pool, with a gymnasium, squash courts and an onboard Post Office, capable of dealing with thousands of items of mail, because the mail was as important as passengers on the North Atlantic route from Britain to America.

Everything about the new ships would be a superlative. They were fully a third larger than *Lusitania* and *Mauretania*, and they would have the largest reciprocating engines ever built. They were simply titanic in size and their names reflected this confidence from their builders: *Olympic* was to be the first ship, her first sister would be *Titanic* and the third vessel was to be *Gigantic*. Each one would be a triumph of the shipbuilder's art and each would, in turn, confirm Harland & Wolff's position as the premier builder of ocean liners in the world. *Olympic* and *Titanic* would be built side by side under the new Arrol Gantry, designed and built by the same firm that had built the Forth Railway Bridge. The Arrol Gantry was 840 feet long, 228 feet high and was 270 feet wide. It was equipped with moving cranes and huge ramps up each side, to be used as the ships were constructed for the steel that would make up the plating on the side of each ship.

The ships themselves would be held together with 4 million rivets, some hammered in by hand but the majority riveted using state-of-the-art machines. On 16 December 1908, after much work at the Queens Island yard, the first plates of steel were laid – the ribs of the keel that everything on *Olympic* would branch from. At 882.6 feet in length, with a width of 92.5 feet, *Olympic* would dwarf anything yet built. Barely a decade before, a ship of half the size was unimaginable and here, Harland & Wolff were making a leap into the unknown, building a series of liners, each slightly larger than the last. With a displacement of 60,000 tons and a gross tonnage of 45,324, they were watched with interest by not only other shipping lines and shipyards, but by the general public too. The press followed the construction with interest and White Star advertised the new ships with gusto. The design was such that leading shipping journals were calling the ships 'practically unsinkable'; a double keel and a series of watertight bulkheads were designed in such a way that five could be damaged and flooded and the ships would still float.

On 20 October 1910, the great and the good travelled to Belfast on special trains and chartered steamships for the launch of the first of the trio. Painted in a light grey to aid the throng of photographers who swarmed around the yard and took up position along the banks of the river, all jostling for the best view, the *Olympic* took to the water. Soon, tugs were swarming around her, pulling her to the fitting-out area, where she would be equipped with her boilers, engines and other machinery; and where she would be fitted out, the bare decks being filled with kitchens, storerooms, bedrooms, public rooms and cargo-handling equipment.

On the day of the launch of *Olympic*, her sister, *Titanic*, a notice board at her bow proclaiming her name and build number of SS 401, was still part plated but she would soon be ready for launching too. The steelworkers and rivetters would be diverted to her, while on board *Olympic*, the carpenters, plumbers, electricians and engineers took over. About six months or so behind *Olympic*, *Titanic* took to the water on 31 May 1910, the same day her sister was handed over to White Star and left Belfast for her first journey to Liverpool and Southampton. That day a record was made: Belfast harbour had over 100,000 tons of shipping in port, 90 per cent of that in two vessels. Many guests had toured *Olympic* in the morning, proclaiming their amazement at the sheer luxury of the new vessel, before viewing the launch of her mighty sister. *Olympic* would have only the second swimming pool ever fitted to an ocean liner, she had electric lifts, the latest in equipment as well as sumptuous suites and Third Class accommodation that was better than many a ship's First Class areas. *Olympic* was a floating wonder and Bruce Ismay proclaimed that her sisters would be even more luxurious.

The *Olympic* and *Titanic* were the talk of the world. The publicity machine had been working overtime for months before *Olympic* entered service. She had been branded 'the ship magnificent' and all of the company's brochures, menus for Second and Third Classes and letterheads stated the company was building the 'largest steamers in the world, over 45,000 tons'. Postcards were issued of the new liners, cigarette and chocolate tins advertised them; even boxes of matches mentioned the new ships.

The London & South Western Railway, owner of the port of Southampton, had been constructing a new dock for the ships on reclaimed land close to the town's Royal Pier. It was a major undertaking and work had started soon after the announcement that White Star was building the superliners. Work had not been completed before *Olympic*'s maiden arrival in the port on 2 June 1911, after a brief stop at Liverpool to show the vessel off there.

Olympic was a superlative vessel; the world's longest, largest, widest and tallest – but not the fastest, nor was she intended to be anything but a luxurious and comfortable travelling hotel. Her maiden voyage left Southampton on 14 June 1911 and was completed in five days, sixteen hours and forty-two minutes at a speed of 21.17 kt. On the maiden return voyage T. O. M. Sopwith, the famous aviator, flew over the ship, dropping some forgotten spectacles to a passenger. Despite the sheer size of *Olympic*, he missed and the glasses were lost in the Hudson forever.

Olympic soon proved herself to be comfortable and free of major vibration. However, her sheer size proved a challenge and it was to cause a major incident that would see her 'practically unsinkable' reputation come under scrutiny. In September 1911, outward bound on her fifth voyage, she was rammed by HMS *Hawke*, a cruiser, and severely holed both above and below the waterline. It was an accident that caused delays in the construction of her almost-identical sister, *Titanic*, pushing her maiden voyage back, and ultimately leading to the loss of *Titanic*.

The North German Lloyd steamer *Kaiser Wilhelm der Grosse*, first of the four-stackers, at Cherbourg, having been involved in a collision with the Royal Mail Steam Packet Company ship *Orinoco*.

Above: The *Deutschland* in dry dock, showing the sleek lines of the German ships.

Right: Lord Pirrie (right).

Below: Launch of the *Oceanic* at Harland & Wolff's, the first of a series of ever-larger White Star Line vessels intended to compete with the German ships.

T.S.S. Mauretania

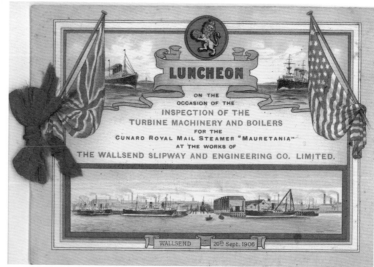

LUNCHEON

ON THE
OCCASION OF THE
INSPECTION OF THE
TURBINE MACHINERY AND BOILERS
FOR THE
Cunard Royal Mail Steamer "Mauretania"
AT THE WORKS OF
THE WALLSEND SLIPWAY AND ENGINEERING CO. LIMITED.

WALLSEND   20th Sept. 1906

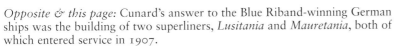

Opposite & this page: Cunard's answer to the Blue Riband-winning German ships was the building of two superliners, *Lusitania* and *Mauretania*, both of which entered service in 1907.

Opposite, clockwise from far left: Lusitania in dry dock at Liverpool, prior to her maiden voyage.

Mauretania having her funnels installed at Wallsend.

Mr and Mrs Swan's menu for inspection of the engines and machinery of the *Mauretania* at Wallsend.

This page, from top left: Lusitania running her speed trials off Ailsa Craig.

Ready for her maiden voyage, *Lusitania* at the Landing Stage.

The Verandah Lounge of *Mauretania* in a rare 1907 colour view by the Locomotive Publishing Company, which issued two cards of the ship.

Typical of their period, the two items on this page are what passengers would have received aboard ship. On the left is the cover of a passenger list of 1919, when Commander Arthur H. Rostron was captain of *Mauretania* on one of her early post-war voyages. On the right is a First Class Menu from *Lusitania*'s pre-war service. Both are highly decorative.

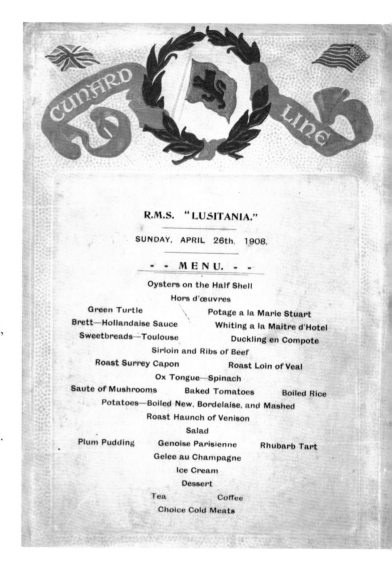

SCENE ON THE RIVER MERSEY LIVERPOOL~ MARCH 7TH 1914

Clockwise from top left: Lusitania approached the Stage, anchor down, prior to her maiden voyage.

A Mersey Docks & Harbour Board postcard showing *Mauretania* in March 1914.

The new gantry at Harland & Wolff, with much of the metal for *Titanic* and *Olympic* in the foreground.

The *Olympic*-class ships were well represented in art form.

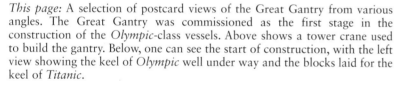

BELFAST.
QUEEN'S ISLAND

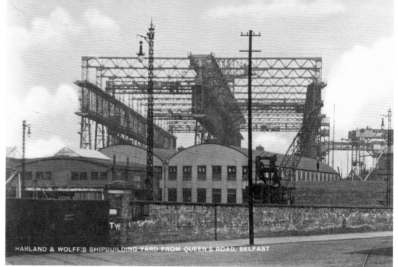

HARLAND & WOLFF'S SHIPBUILDING YARD FROM QUEEN'S ROAD, BELFAST

This page: A selection of postcard views of the Great Gantry from various angles. The Great Gantry was commissioned as the first stage in the construction of the *Olympic*-class vessels. Above shows a tower crane used to build the gantry. Below, one can see the start of construction, with the left view showing the keel of *Olympic* well under way and the blocks laid for the keel of *Titanic*.

The Gantry, Harland & Wolff, Belfast.

Liner on Stocks, Harland & Wolff's Shipyard, Belfast.

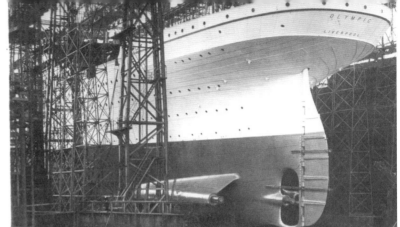

"OLYMPIC" (THE STERN) IN THE SLIP

This page: A selection of postcard views of the two ships under construction. *Olympic* was painted in an all-over light grey to ensure photographs of her would show the detail of her construction. The above views show her almost ready for launching. Below, right, is a view taken from *Olympic* after her launch looking across to the Great Gantry with *Titanic* still on the stocks. Two local publishers, Hurst and Walton, did many postcard views of the ships under construction.

Above: A rare view of *Olympic* in the Thompson Graving Dock. Note the toilets on her poop deck, built out over the side of the ship.

Below: *Olympic* is almost complete, with scaffolding around her aft funnels in a view looking across the river.

Above: Olympic enters Southampton for the very first time, June 1911.

Below: Olympic is dressed overall in flags in this unique postcard view of her while open for public inspection ar Southampton prior to her maiden voyage.

Chapter Two

BUILDING THE SHIPS

A century ago, history was made when the *Titanic* sank on her maiden voyage. It took 15,000 men to build her and her sister ship, *Olympic*, both built side by side on slips 2 and 3 at Harland & Wolff's Belfast yard.

In 1907, Harland & Wolff began the rebuilding of their Queens Island, Belfast, yard, located on the River Lagan. Three slipways were rebuilt into a double slip, under a huge gantry, which was designed by Sir William Arrol, who had designed and constructed the Forth Railway Bridge. The gantry was to become a familiar Belfast landmark for many years and underneath its 840 feet x 240 feet were two slipways. The gantry was 228 feet high and had numerous cranes, as well as four lifts and inclined walkways. The gantry dominated the Belfast skyline until the 1960s, when it was demolished and replaced by *Samson* and *Goliath*, the two yellow cranes that now dominate Queens Island. As well as the new gantry, construction began on a new dry dock, the largest in Britain.

The two new slipways were strengthened with reinforced concrete which was 4 feet 6 inches thick. *Olympic* was built in Slip 2 and *Titanic* was built in Slip 3, her keel being laid on 31 March 1909.

It was the building of this gantry and the new dry dock that signified that something huge was happening in Belfast. Soon, it was announced that the White Star Line was building two new liners, to be named *Olympic* and *Titanic*. They would be fully 50 per cent larger than the next largest – the *Mauretania* and *Lusitania*, both of which entered service in 1907. White Star was sending a message to the world's shipping lines that they were the most important transatlantic line.

At any one time, up to 15,000 men were working in the Belfast yard, most of them on the two giant superliners. Harland & Wolff was unique in that almost every skill to fabricate a ship was available in house. The company had huge engine works and sawmills at Belfast, as well as buildings for carpenters, electricians and a foundry too.

When work began on *Titanic*, she was already three months behind *Olympic*, whose keel was laid on 16 December 1908. She was totally framed by the middle of April 1910, while

Olympic had been fully plated by then. The frames were the ribs of the ship, while the plates could be imagined as being the skin. Each piece of steel was carefully cut and bent to make it fit the specific part of the ship it was to be located in. The moulds or templates for the iron and steel work were made in the moulding loft. The shell plates or sheets of steel would then be heated in the foundry and bent to conform to the moulds and templates constructed. Many of the photographs of the yard show the great gantry and the area around it, stacked with sheet steel, upwards of an inch thick, ready to be used in the plating of the ships.

The great gantry, as well as cranes, had huge riveting machines, which were used to hammer in the majority of the 4 million rivets used in the ship's construction, while some of the areas inaccessible to the huge machine would be riveted by teams of men, on either side of the sheet steel, all paid on piece work. Foremen would check the quality of the riveting and tallymen would count the rivets so the teams of riveters could get paid for their work.

Olympic was launched on 29 October 1910 and the men who had been outfitting her transferred back to *Titanic*, finishing off her shell plating and beginning to prepare the inside spaces for the fitment of the boiler, engines and turbine that were under construction in the engine and boiler works. As well as work in the yard, work was being undertaken elsewhere. The propellers were being cast in London, the stern frame manufactured in Darlington, the anchors and anchor chain in Netherton, the lifeboat davits in Brierley Hill and the ship's bells in Liverpool.

The launch of the ship took place on 31 May 1911, taking 62 seconds to make her first journey into the water. Riding high in the water, she bobbed around as she was cut free of the drag chains and shepherded by tugs. *Titanic* was towed from the end of the slipway to the fitting out area, which was located next to the new Thompson dry dock, which was officially opened on 1 April 1911 and was the largest dry dock in the world at the time. The dry dock, first used by the *Olympic* for hull cleaning and painting, could be pumped dry of 21 million gallons of water in 1 hour and 40 minutes. There was one accident on launch day, when an employee named James Dobbins was mortally wounded by some falling timbers, dying the next day. He was not the first to die when the ship was being built, five others being killed while working on the ship and two in the works when constructing parts of the ship. In comparison, nine people died during the construction of *Olympic*.

Harland & Wolff had also purchased a large floating crane from Germany in 1911 at a cost of £30,000 and it was used to lift the boilers, engines, funnels and other large assemblies into place. The engines themselves had been built up in the engine works and tested, before being disassembled and then fitted aboard the ship itself.

Titanic varied slightly from *Olympic* but the most visible changes did not take place until she was almost fitted out, and ready to sail. Thomas Andrews, one of her designers, had travelled extensively on *Olympic* and made copious notes of alterations to make to the next in the class. Bruce Ismay, chairman of White Star, had also considered alterations. The most visible of these were on A and B decks, with an enclosed promenade and a new series of cabins too, each with their own private veranda.

The men of Harland & Wolff knew they were building something special – at the time of the launch of *Titanic*, *Olympic* had just been completed and Belfast held the record for shipping tonnage in dock. The ships were the largest ever seen to date, the most luxurious, and had been built with no expense spared. After an extensive period outfitting, during which *Olympic* had visited the yard for repairs to her stern and for a dropped propeller blade, *Titanic* was finally ready for her maiden voyage in April 1912. She left the yard on 2 April, with workmen still finishing off many of her cabins and public spaces. After successful sea trials she sailed for Southampton, where the men of Harland & Wolff's yard there would finish her off. Despite the delay in her maiden voyage, some areas had not been completed by the time of the maiden voyage on 10 April. The heating in parts of the ship was non-existent, in others it was too high, while the ship had been filled with flowers to disguise the smells of fresh paint and varnish. Nine employees of Harland & Wolff, including Thomas Andrews, sailed on the maiden voyage as a guarantee group, checking over everything, fixing any little snags, and generally ensuring the ship was perfect in every way. Sadly, none were to survive the sinking and they brought the total number of Harland & Wolff men who died during the building of the ship to seventeen.

Titanic's loss was a tragedy for Belfast and for Harland & Wolff. Now, a full century after the disaster, Belfast has come to terms with the loss and is celebrating the ship for the engineering triumph that it was. A large area in Queens Island is being redeveloped as the *Titanic* Quarter and a museum is due to open this year, dedicated to the *Titanic* and the men who built her. To quote a shipyard employee of the time, 'we just builds 'em, and shove 'em in'. It sums up well the attitude of the 15,000 men who built *Titanic*.

Standing in front of *Olympic* are just a very small sample of the 15,000 men and boys who built the two sister ships. This view was taken some point in May 1912, prior to *Olympic*'s departure for Liverpool and Southampton. These proud men had helped to create the world's largest ships, fully one third larger than the next largest competitors, *Mauretania* and *Lusitania*.

Giant Floating Crane, Harland & Wolff's, Belfast.

Harland and Wolff's Shipyard Belfast

Left: Published by Walton, of Belfast, but also available in a Reliable Series postcard, this view shows the secondhand floating crane bought from Germany to enable the construction of the two superliners. It is moving a huge casting for *Olympic, c.* 1910.

Right, above: Looking from the bow of *Olympic* towards the main buildings at Harland & Wolff, this is just some of her steel plating in the foreground.

Right, below: Titanic is almost ready for launching as thousands of workers stream away from Harland & Wolff after a hard day's work. On the left is the *Nomadic*, already complete and ready to sail with *Olympic* on 31 May 1911.

Above: The classic view of the Great Gantry, published by Valentine of Dundee.

Above: Olympic and *Titanic* on the launch day of *Olympic*.

Below: On another Valentine card, *Olympic* is seen entering the water for the first time.

Below: Olympic enters the Thompson Graving Dock for the first time, with crowds on either side of the new dock.

THE NEW DRY DOCK AND "OLYMPIC," BELFAST.

Clockwise, from top left: A rare postcard view of *Olympic* being fitted out, with the new Thompson Graving Dock in the foreground.

Titanic's central anchor on its way from Noah Hingley's in Netherton. Hingley's would manufacture all of the anchors for the *Olympic*-class vessels and teams of heavy horses would haul them away from their Black Country foundry to Fleetwood, for transport across the Irish Sea. Interestingly, the Black Country Living Museum has some of the anchor chain from the ships, which was used to test the breaking strain.

Olympic has almost entered the new Graving Dock in this Walton postcard.

Above: This postcard gives an idea of the size of the central anchor of the three ships. This was a unique Hingley design. A postcard exists simply entitled 'Black Country Industries, Anchor Making', which shows this anchor too.

Below: Titanic's central anchor being loaded at Fleetwood for onward travel to Belfast.

Above: The Great Gantry. This is probably *Titanic* under construction, with plating up as high as C deck.

Below: The Donegal Quay, close to Queen's Island, where dignitaries for the launch of *Olympic*, *Titanic* and *Britannic* would be disembarked.

Above and below: Two views showing the launch of the *Titanic*. Despite a huge number of people coming to view the launch and departure of *Olympic*, postcards of the launch are rare. The below view is taken from the opposite side of the Lagan.

Above: One of many postcards issued, advertising the scale and sheer presence of the *Olympic*-class vessels.

Below: Another view of the launch of the *Titanic*, taken from the end of Slips 2 and 3.

THE LAUNCH OF THE S.S. TITANIC MAY 31. 1911

THE WHITE STAR LINER TITANIC 45,000 TONS.
SUCCESSFULLY LAUNCHED AT BELFAST MAY 31ST 1911.

THE S. S. "OLYMPIC" LEAVING BELFAST FOR LIVERPOOL.
THE WORLD'S BIGGEST SHIP.

Above and below: After the launch of *Titanic*, the *Olympic* left for Liverpool and Southampton. At both places she was opened up to the public for inspection, as she had been at Belfast. She is shown below at Southampton and the as yet incomplete White Star Dock, and dressed overall in flags. Note the lighters along her port side, filling her with coal in preparation for her maiden voyage.

Above: Titanic being fitted out. This is close to her being completed and painted in her final coat of paint.

Below: It is possible to work out when certain images of *Olympic* were published due to the gross tonnage displayed on the postcards, such as this company-issued one. Showing her near New York, this is a 1920s view.

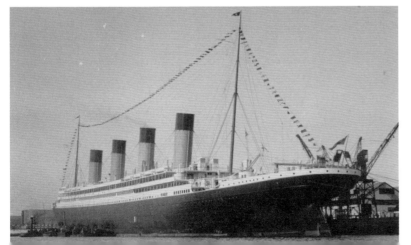

WHITE STAR LINE.

TRIPLE-SCREW R.M.S. "OLYMPIC,"
46,439 TONS,
THE LARGEST BRITISH STEAMER,
PASSING AMBROSE CHANNEL LIGHTSHIP.

Chapter Three

PRACTICALLY UNSINKABLE

'As far as it is possible to do so, these two wonderful vessels are designed to be unsinkable.' White Star publicity brochure, 1911

The White Star Line had proclaimed the safety of their brand new ships *Olympic* and *Titanic*, mentioning their ability to float even if four watertight compartments had been breached. The double bottom and specially-designed watertight doors all aided the illusion of their invincibility. The line's faith in the vessels would be put to the test on *Olympic*'s fifth westbound voyage on 20 September 1911.

Captain Edward John Smith had been transferred to the *Olympic* from the line's older *Adriatic*. He was the most experienced captain of the fleet but no one had experience of such large vessels, *Olympic* being fully a third larger than the next largest ships, *Mauretania* and *Lusitania*. It was discovered very quickly that such large vessels as *Olympic* could cause problems in shallow water due to the thrust from their propellers. This suction had a nasty habit of pulling vessels towards the huge liner. This had first been demonstrated during *Olympic*'s maiden arrival into New York on 21 June 1911, when the tug *O.L.* *Hallenbach* was unceremoniously damaged after she was sucked into the side of the huge vessel during docking manoeuvres.

Fast-forwarding to 20 September, *Olympic* set sail for the New World as normal, but today would not be like any other day. It would blemish Captain Smith's career, losing him his $1,000 crash bonus for 1911, but at the same time helping the ship's reputation as being unsinkable. The ship left for New York at 11.10 a.m. with over 1,300 passengers while HMS *Hawke*, a cruiser, had left Portsmouth with Commander W. F. Blunt in charge. Little did Captains Smith and Blunt know they were on a collision course that would alter history forever.

To try and describe the course changes each ship took would take a little while, but the basic gist of the matter is that the *Olympic* and *Hawke* spent some time pacing each other in the Solent off the Bramble Shoal, which entailed *Olympic* making a reverse S-turn. She had started to pick up speed by 12.46 and was accelerating along up to her coastal maximum speed of 20 knots. *Hawke*'s captain had first spotted *Olympic* on his return from lunch at 12.37 and by 12.41 *Hawke* was making 15 knots, with

Olympic making 11 and getting faster. Technically, *Hawke* was the overtaking vessel and should keep clear of *Olympic*. Then *Hawke* began to turn, heading for *Olympic*. Blunt ordered 'hard a port', yet his ship continued to turn towards *Olympic*. The engines were ordered astern but still she continued travelling forward.

The pilot, Bowyer, realising she was about to hit, ordered the helm hard over. Slowly, *Olympic* turned away from *Hawke*, but it was too late, and with a resounding crash, *Hawke*'s reinforced bow slammed into the stern of the liner. The watertight doors were ordered closed as *Olympic* started to settle by the stern. *Hawke* was more severely damaged – only the swift action of her crew kept her afloat. Pumps working at full stretch and with mats across the damaged bow, she limped back to Portsmouth.

Olympic was stopped and the damage inspected. Two watertight compartments were breached and totally flooded, another partially, there was a 40-foot tear below the waterline, with a gaping hole into Second Class accommodation above it. It was obvious she was going nowhere. Her starboard propeller had been damaged and there was a fear that the shaft was out of alignment. She remained overnight, while some of her passengers left for Liverpool and the line's *Adriatic* for New York. Towed back into Southampton the next morning, she returned to her berth and the damage was checked over. Divers checked her under the waterline, the men from Harland & Wolff's in Southampton started repairs. The temporary repairs would take a fortnight. Wood patched up the holes, concrete was used to temporarily repair some of the holes below the waterline. She limped to Belfast on one engine and further repairs took five weeks. Those repairs were to take many hundreds of men away from *Titanic*, and delay her maiden voyage.

Six weeks after arriving back at Belfast, and at huge cost to White Star, *Olympic* left again to re-enter service. She had proved herself practically unsinkable, for a smaller ship would have been cut in two and lost. In February 1912, *Olympic* would return again to Belfast after losing a propeller blade. *Titanic* was hauled out of dry dock and it would be the last time the ships would be in port together. Both Bruce Ismay and Thomas Andrews, the designer of the ships, had been aboard *Olympic* and taken copious notes on the workings of the ship and set about to add improvements into the design of *Titanic*. Some of these were done at an early stage but the major external difference between the two ships, the enclosed promenade deck, was not completed until quite late in *Titanic*'s fitting out. It wasn't until late March that the promenade deck was plated over and windows added.

A naval enquiry put the blame entirely on *Olympic*. The White Star Line were not even represented and they counter-sued. A court battle ensued and the 'suction theory' came into being. The large superliners required a different kind of handling and care had to be taken close to other vessels. The judgement recorded that *Olympic* was to blame due to faulty navigation and costs were awarded to the Admiralty. The final judgement came long after the *Hawke* herself had been sunk and a full two years after Captain Smith's death when one of his supposedly unsinkable ships sank!

Olympic herself was repaired, although some argue she and *Titanic* were swapped in some huge insurance fiddle after the damage caused by the *Hawke* to *Olympic*'s stern casting and propeller shafts. What the collision did show was the effects that 50,000 tons of displacement and huge propellers had on other ships close by, something that would be seen within the year, on *Titanic*'s maiden voyage, when her departure from Southampton pulled the SS *New York* from the dockside.

Hawke was lost in 1914, torpedoed in the North Sea by U-9 on 15 October. She sank in five minutes. *Olympic*, despite the damage, went on to become one of White Star's most successful vessels. Her captain, however, went down in history as the man who sailed the *Titanic* into an iceberg, at the time the only floating object with a larger displacement than a White Star *Olympic*-class ship.

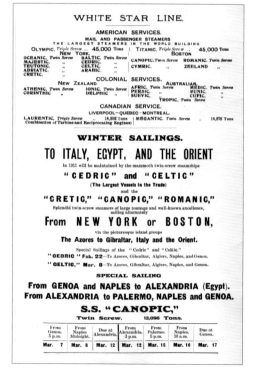

THE COLLISION BETWEEN H.M.S.HAWKE & S.S.OLYMPIC OFF COWES SEP 20 1911.

Right: Two postcards illustrating the ramming of the *Olympic* by HMS *Hawke*. Postcards of the event and its aftermath are not uncommon, but no photographic postcards are known of the collision between the two vessels. Photographers such as Reginald Silk and Stephen Cribb, of Portsmouth, did long series of the damage to the two vessels, with images of *Hawke* at Portsmouth and *Olympic* at Southampton, with divers at her side.

Collision between H.M.S. Hawke White Star liner Olympic off Cowes 20th Sep 1911

Left: This unique postcard, a private one showing an unknown lady on the beach near Cowes, Isle of Wight, is important for illustrating the *Olympic* stopped and awaiting tugs after the ramming. A Red Funnel steamer crowded with people is ready to pass close by the stricken liner.

Right: The gash in the side of *Olympic* extended far below the waterline too. A diver is underwater examining the damage.

Left: Crowds look on at the damage to *Olympic*, with the salvage men busy at work in the foreground. *Olympic* was repaired with wood and concrete and sailed for Belfast, the only dry dock big enough to accommodate her.

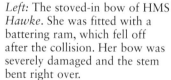

HMS 'HAWKE'
SHOWING HER BATTERED BOWS
AFTER THE COLLISION WITH THE OLYMPIC

Left: The stoved-in bow of HMS *Hawke.* She was fitted with a battering ram, which fell off after the collision. Her bow was severely damaged and the stem bent right over.

Right, above: This is one of the rarer views of the disaster by Cribb, showing *Olympic* returning to Berth 43 at Southampton Docks, and with the damage to her stern marked out. Repairing her was the start of a slippery slope for the moving of the maiden voyage of her sister.

Right, below: Another Stephen Cribb view of HMS *Hawke* being returned to Portsmouth.

HMS HAWKE after COLLISION with OLYMPIC 20 Sept 1911

Left, above: With crash matting and tarpaulins draped over her bow, *Hawke* arrives back at Portsmouth.

Left, below: A card issued both pre and post sinking of *Titanic*. On the lettering the gaps made by removing all evidence of *Titanic* are quite visible. This company-issued postcard is one of the rare period artist-drawn postcards that shows both vessels. Note the *Titanic* sailing into the distance.

WHITE STAR LINE.

"OLYMPIC." 45,000 TONS. AND "TITANIC." 45,000 TONS. THE LARGEST STEAMERS IN THE WORLD.

ALL STEAMERS BUILT IN IRELAND.

QUEENSTOWN—NEW YORK
ON THURSDAYS AND FRIDAYS.

QUEENSTOWN—BOSTON
ON WEDNESDAYS.

For Freight and Passage apply to

JOHN DENNEHY,

Insurance Agent, CAHIRCIVEEN, Co. Kerry

Chapter Four

FIRST CLASS

It was First Class that made *Titanic* special. She had been built with no expense spared for luxury. Her builders had been instructed on a cost plus basis, and the final cost had been $7.5 million, or about £2 million. A suite aboard cost £870 ($4,350), or about £60,000 in today's money. A much more basic First Class berth was £30 (or about £2,000 today), while a Second Class passage was £12 (or about £800/$1,200) and a Third Class ticket ranged from £3 to £8 (£200 to £500 in today's money). A Third Class ticket price varied depending on the accommodation. For single men, it meant a dormitory, for married families, a cabin.

But, back to First Class and its millionaires' suites. First Class on *Titanic* was by far and away the most salubrious on the Atlantic. White Star had given in trying to have the fastest ship on the route, wisely going for luxury and size as the selling points of their vessels. *Titanic* did not disappoint – she was truly the most magnificent of vessels, having only the third swimming pool aboard any ocean liner, a squash court, gymnasium and glamorous public rooms, including a Café Parisien, à la carte restaurant, a sumptuous smoking room and the finest staircase afloat, crowned by a huge glass dome and with a clock, surrounded by a carved sculpture of 'Honour and Glory Crowning Time'.

Unlike her sister *Olympic*, *Titanic*'s B Deck had extra cabins added, including two parlour suites, each with its own 50-foot promenade. The First Class Restaurant was enlarged, and, on her starboard side, a Café Parisien was added. The A Deck was fitted with an enclosed promenade area as this area on *Olympic* suffered in bad weather, showering the passengers in sea water and rain in the worst Atlantic storms. The alterations to A and B decks gave *Titanic* a gross tonnage of 46,328 tons, fully 1,004 tons larger than her sister, making her the largest moving object in the world. Much of this size was devoted to First Class accommodations and public areas.

The numerous suites and cabins were finished in a variety of styles from Louis XIV and Adam, with many provided with private bathrooms, which were still a novelty on the open sea. First Class was meant to equal the world's best hotels and it did. From the luxurious promenade suites to the smaller cabins for one or two, the ship's accommodation did not disappoint.

"OLYMPIC" RESTAURANT.

This page, clockwise from above: Many postcards were issued both by the White Star Line and commercial publishers of the interiors of the first two *Olympic*-class vessels. Many used photographs taken by Harland & Wolff photographer Robert Welch, such as the two above, while others were taken from company artwork such as the colour view of the restaurant on *Olympic* shown to the right. Publishers of interior views included C. R. Hoffmann, who had a shop at the entrance to Southampton Docks, and Ocean Trading Co., of Southampton. Note the absence of any china and silverware in the two photographs. These images were taken when *Olympic* was still at Belfast and her china and silverware was probably yet to arrive. No such problems with the art card issued by the company of the restaurant.

On board S.S. "MEGANTIC."

Aug 5— 1911

"OLYMPIC" (46,000 TONS) & "TITANIC" (45,000 TONS)
LARGEST STEAMERS IN THE WORLD.
(50 LINES)

Dear Goosie,

Two letters in one day. This boat is fine, new, & well equipped throughout. no motion or vibration noticeable. Wouldn't hardly know you were moving — A pleasant company on board — 107 first class passengers. The food is excellent & abundant, and in great variety. Shall have to look that I do not gain — The manager of line is on board, and has searched us out, and evidently we shall get special attention

Nellie took only one trunk besides her hat trunk & a suit case - Bert is in good spirits & looks better than when he was in France. & apparently is care free. River view is not like the maine rivers or the Hudson, so too wide, & county too level & not much settled on shores. We are on river three days 936 miles —

Ask Hospital if I got Smiths name right.
Dr. Poor asked for bill. When Bob makes out bills,

in case of doubt, leave it. I am especially anxious you should get a rest. I have also asked George to look you over, & see if you need any thing for more than a rest. Charley says he is much better. They were in Boston only one day, & tried to go out. Rusty looked well, but was very thin. It was so hot in Montreal last night that a sprinkling cart took fire from spontaneous combustion. — Wish you would send the news having account

of town meeting to me in London.
You go down to nantucket without me. - There is no doubt of your welcome.
Also run that car, & get your license the first thing. In case of serious sickness go to the Hospital - In case of other sickness have Geo, & Wass. Tell Van to look out for him. You wont hear again now till the other side.
With much love
Lewis

Above: As the ships were under construction all of the company advertising and letterheads proclaimed the building of the two largest ships in the world. This letter, sent from the brand new *Megantic*, on the Canadian run, gives a flavour of the quality of service. The writer notes that the manager of the line, Bruce Ismay, is on board and had searched them out.

This page: A variety of press images and artist's impressions of the public rooms of an *Olympic*-class vessel. All of these areas offered a quality and space previously unseen at sea. The large, spacious gymnasium of *Olympic* contrasts nicely with the First Class Smoking Room, with painting by Norman Wilkinson over the fireplace, the luxurious grand staircase and the garden lounge, with its wicker chairs and bright, airy outlook onto deck.

This page: Two different views of two different rooms aboard both *Olympic* and *Titanic*. Looking into the ship, the garden lounge is shown. Below and above, right are the Turkish Baths of both ships. *Olympic*'s is below and the colour view shows that of *Titanic*. This was one area in which both ships had different designs and decor.

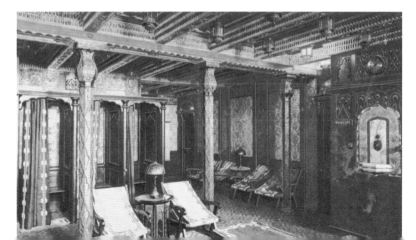

This page: Cabins aboard an *Olympic*-class vessel. Many of the photographs taken by Harland & Wolff's official photographer, Robert Welch, show cabins from aboard *Olympic*. Welch was the son of a gifted Scottish photographer and was born in Strabane, County Tyrone, on 22 July 1859. His photographs of Ireland and Irish life are world renowned but it is his photographs of *Olympic* and *Titanic* under construction that he is most famous for. He died on 28 September 1936.

The First Class cabins aboard *Olympic* and *Titanic* varied greatly in style, and in size, with some cabins being parts of connecting suites, while some also had private bathrooms. The cabins had to appeal to the varied tastes of the passengers, who were, after all, from different parts of the world, with different ideas on décor. The cabins here were all on B-deck and these photographs are primarily of cabins aboard *Olympic*. Robert Welch photographed almost every part of the *Olympic* during her construction, from the double bottom to the tops of her funnels and every public space and many cabins were well documented. The cabins themselves were not created in situ but were prefabricated. Some were created in Belfast, others were made in Harland & Wolff's works in Southampton and even the wood-working company of H. H. Martyn, of Cheltenham, created some of the interiors. Every cabin was made up and then each part was stenciled so that it could be dismantled and then reassembled aboard the liner.

Opposite page, clockwise from top left: Cabin B58, in the style of Louis XVI.

A Queen Anne-style cabin, this is B60.

B64 was in the Empire style.

When people talk of a conspiracy and that the *Olympic* and *Titanic* were switched, they do not consider that this could only have been done over a period of a week and that every item aboard each ship had to be swapped over, or that 15,000 Harland & Wolff workers had to be sworn to secrecy and that none of them would ever talk about the switch. Every panel that has ever come up for sale from the *Olympic* (and there are lots) has been stenciled or stamped SS400 – her unique Harland & Wolff build number. One or two items recovered from the wreck scene of the *Titanic* are stenciled SS401. Bearing in mind the months of labour needed to fit out the ships, it is highly unlikely that the swap could have been done in such a short time.

This page, clockwise from top left: B59 in the Old Dutch style.

B57 was in a Modern Dutch style.

The swimming pool aboard Olympic. Inside the ship on Deck E, this was one of the very first purpose-built swimming pools aboard a ship. By the time Hamburg Amerika Line's *Imperator* came into service in 1913, the Spartan look was gone and marble and tiles were definitely in favour.

Chapter Five

SECOND CLASS

Second Class also saw some changes due to the experiences of *Olympic*. Still opulent, certainly in comparison to many other ocean liners, *Titanic* was the pinnacle of Edwardian luxury, with the first electric elevator for Second Class passengers fitted to an ocean-going vessel. Notable Second Class passengers included an English schoolteacher called Lawrence Beesley, who had been photographed by photographers of the *Illustrated London News* on the day of sailing while in the gymnasium. He would go on to write a book about the disaster.

The Second Class accommodations were not as fine as those in First Class but were still luxurious. The dining room was set with long rows of tables rather than the individual tables found in First Class but the Second Class boat deck area was probably the finest on the ship, being located close to the gymnasium. This area would be the scene of high drama as the events of the night of the sinking would unfold.

There were still areas of Second Class unfinished during the maiden voyage, with the heating causing havoc. Some cabins were far too hot and others barely above freezing. The novel design of the taps in the bathrooms was also causing issues for some passengers and crew but by the third day of the voyage, those were minor

irritations for some. The lift, although a novelty, did ensure that many passengers visited parts of the ship they otherwise would not have. Beesley's comments were that 'whatever else may have been superfluous, lifts certainly were not. Old ladies, for example, in cabins on F deck would hardly have got to the top deck during the whole voyage had they not been able to ring for the lift boy.' He further went on to say that nothing gave a greater impression of the sheer scale of *Titanic* than taking the lift to the various floors and watching the passengers enter and leave the lift.

Above: The boat deck of *Olympic*. This illustration appears in both White Star brochures of the ships and in the July 1911 issue of G. A. Sekon's *Railway & Travel Monthly*.

Above, right: The Second Class Smoking Room aboard *Olympic*.

Right: The interior of a Second Class cabin aboard *Olympic* and *Titanic*.

Opposite: Titanic being loaded with cargo and supplies prior to her maiden voyage. The large crane is loading into her forward hold. Within this hold was a brand new Renault car, which was lost in the sinking.

Far left and above: This postcard, hand dispatched by the Penzance agent in August 1912, was sent to Ada Bailey, the sister of a *Titanic* victim, to inform her that her parents, who had travelled to New York that month aboard *Oceanic*, had arrived safely. Her brother, Percy Bailey, was also originally booked onto the *Oceanic* in April 1912, and was heading for Akron, Ohio, to be apprenticed to a butcher there. Travelling Second Class aboard *Titanic* on ticket no. 29108, he sent his parents a postcard from Southampton and a letter from Queenstown.

Left: A poster advertising *Titanic*'s maiden voyage.

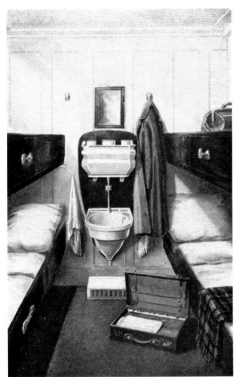

This page: A selection of Second Class bedrooms. Note the rather austere walls, basically no more than painted bulkheads. While some First Class cabins had private bathrooms, those in Second Class had only basic sinks. Many of these were not even connected to the plumbing. The steward would fill them with water and the waste would be removed when the cabin was tidied each day.

Chapter Six

THIRD CLASS

The money-maker on any transatlantic ocean liner was not the First Class accommodation but rather the Third Class or Steerage. Emigrants to North America flooded out of Europe, escaping political and religious persecution in Eastern Europe, or just searching for a better life and new start. From Sweden, Norway, Turkey, France, the United Kingdom and numerous other countries, they made their way to Southampton, Cherbourg and Queenstown (now Cobh) to join the world's largest ship. On some ships, a straw mattress in a dormitory was the height of luxury. For *Titanic* passengers, even those in Third Class, the ship was the ultimate in luxury.

The space that those in Third Class took up represented a small proportion of the passenger space of the ship. Second Class passengers had a huge expanse of the boat deck to use while those in Third Class were kept to the stern of the ship, where they could use the poop deck and the well deck forward of it. The well deck was an area more used to cargo than passengers and large cranes built by Stothert & Pitt in Bath dominated this area. It must not be forgotten that passengers were not *Titanic*'s only cargo. The ship was designed to carry thousands of tons of

goods too and on her maiden voyage those included such things as a Renault car and a precious book, studded with precious jewels. *Titanic* had left Southampton with a relatively small Third Class complement but picked up emigrants from many nations in Cherbourg, including Syrians, East Europeans and families from Western Europe too. The two passenger tenders at Cherbourg were the *Nomadic* and the *Traffic*, which had been built in 1911 and had accompanied *Olympic* from the shipyard. *Nomadic* was intended for First Class passengers while *Traffic*, the smaller ship, was used to take Third Class passengers and luggage to the ships in Cherbourg's outer harbour. *Titanic* would load more human cargo in Queenstown from the tenders *Ireland* and *America*.

Third Class accommodation was spartan, as can be seen from the images opposite. The cabins had cheap pine walls, instead of the opulent satinwood, mahogany, oak and fine wallpapers of First and Second Classes, while the dining room and other lounges had bare metal walls, painted white. Instead of fine art on the walls, images of the company's fleet sufficed. Food, however, was good, although the choice was much more limited. A typical day's fare would include a choice of oatmeal porridge and milk, boiled Cambridge sausages, Irish stew and bread and butter for breakfast. Dinner would be barley broth, beef à la mode, lima beans and boiled potatoes, with rice pudding or oranges for pudding. Tea would be Leicester brawn, pickles, fresh bread and butter with a compote of apricots and rice and supper would be simply gruel and cheese. According to the menu, issued as a postcard, 'any complaint respecting the food supplied, want of attention or incivility, should be at once reported to the Purser or Chief Purser.'

This page: Third Class was more austere again. The view to the right shows the poop deck of *Titanic* on the way to Queenstown. This area was the Third Class outside space. The public rooms, were basic and with sparse decoration. The accommodation on both *Olympic* and *Titanic* was, however, far superior to many vessels. Rather than carpets, the floors are tiled in Linoleum tiles.

WHITE STAR LINE
OLYMPIC & TITANIC

THIRD CLASS ACCOMMODATION

THE LARGEST STEAMERS IN THE WORLD

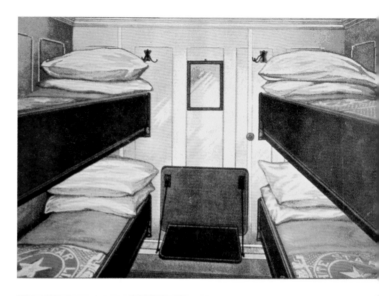

This page: Many postcards were issued pre-sinking of *Titanic*, including this pair (left and below, right) by Raphael Tuck of London. Both classic views of the ships, the printed details on the reverse vary depending on whether the ship had sunk or not. The two designs were very popular both before and after the tragedy but those of the post-sinking cards probably outnumber the earlier version by about fifty to one.

Above, left: A Third Class cabin aboard the *Olympic*-class vessels. This view was published as a postcard in the 1970s.

Chapter Seven

PROVISIONING A GREAT LINER

From *Titanic*'s arrival in Southampton until her departure took a total of eight days. Those days were spent provisioning the ship and preparing her for her maiden voyage. Whole wagon-loads of goods were delivered direct almost to the ship's side, including a prodigious quantity of food, much of which would be consumed on the maiden voyage. Over 7,000 meals were served per day aboard *Titanic*. The table gives an idea of the volume of food consumed aboard on each voyage:

Potatoes	89,600 lb	Sausages	2,500 lb	Apples	6,000
Fresh meat	75,000 lb	Fresh green peas	2,500 lb	Oranges	36,000
Poultry and game	25,000 lb	Coffee	2,200 lb	Lemons	16,000
Fresh fish	11,000 lb	Ice-cream	1,750 lb	Grapefruit	13,000
Rice, dried beans, etc.	10,000 lb	Jams and marmalade	1,120 lb	Ales and stout	15,000 bottles
Sugar	10,000 lb	Grapes	1,000 lb	Minerals	1,200 bottles
Cereals	10,000 lb	Tea	800 lb	Wines	1,000 bottles
Bacon and ham	7,500 lb	Fresh eggs	40,000	Spirits	850 bottles
Fresh butter	6,000 lb	Fresh asparagus	800 bundles	Fresh milk	1,500 gallons
Salt and dried fish	4,000 lb	Lettuce	7,000 heads	Fresh cream	1,200 quarts
Onions	3,500 lb	Sweetbreads	1,000	Condensed milk	600 gallons
Tomatoes	3,500 lb	Flour	250 barrels	Cigars	8,000

As well as food, *Titanic* had to be provisioned with china, silverware, linen and glassware. The china came from various Staffordshire potteries, and the crystal and glassware mainly from Stuart Crystal. Sheffield manufacturers provided much of the silver plate, with Elkington manufacturing thousands of items in its Dubarry pattern for the ship.

In total, there were 57,600 items of china and earthenware, 29,000 pieces of glassware, and 44,000 items of cutlery, each needing stored, ready for use. They were broken down as follows:

The linens for *Titanic* were mostly made in Ireland, and included:

Asparagus Tongs	400	Aprons	4,000
Dinner Plates	12,000	Bath Towels	7,500
Egg Spoons	2,000	Bed Covers	3,600
Finger Bowls	1,000	Blankets	7,500
Grape Scissors	1,500	Double Sheets	3,000
Ice Cream Plates	5,500	Eiderdown Quilts	800
Nut Crackers	300	Fine Towels	25,000
Oyster Forks	1,000	Pillow-slips	15,000
Pudding Dishes	1,200	Roller Towels	3,500
Salt Shakers	2,000	Single Sheets	15,000
Soufflé Dishes	1,500	Table Cloths	6,000
Tea Cups	3,000	Table Napkins	45,000
Wine Glasses	2,000		

Above, left: Many suppliers used images of the company's ships to promote their own goods by association. Moir's provided tea for the *Olympic* and *Titanic*.

Above, middle: A page from a passenger list giving details of services available on board. Each ship had its own printing press, used to issue company notices, passenger lists and menus. The blank passenger lists would be printed ashore but the actual names would be printed on ship, so as to be as accurate as possible.

Above: This view of *Olympic* at Plymouth was painted by Norman Wilkinson and is reputed to be the one that showed 'Plymouth harbour' that hung in the First Class Smoking Room of *Titanic*. Interestingly, Plymouth was a naval port but offered a fast train service to london and so the steamers called there on their way to Southampton. Mail and passengers were carried by special boat train, for which tickets could be bought on board ship. The tender at the side of *Olympic* belonged to the Great Western Railway and also carried the crew of the *Titanic* to Plymouth after the sinking when *Lapland* brough them to the port.

WOMEN'S GUILD OF EMPIRE COMMITTEE.

Left to Right—Miss Waddell (*Sec.*), Mrs. Charlesworth, Mrs. Flora Drummond (*Controller-in-Chief*), Mrs. R. S. Henderson (*President 1924-1926*), Lady Muriel Gore Browne. Miss Bowerman (*Hon. Sec.*).

Elsie Edith Bowerman was a militant suffragette in the pre-First World War period. She and her mother booked cabin E33 aboard *Titanic* on a voyage to the USA and Canada. Rescued on lifeboat six with her mother, she went on to be secretary of the Women's Guild of Empire in the 1920s. She is shown here (far right) in this 1926 postcard. With its suffrage and *Titanic* interest, this is a rare and valuable postcard, issued by the Guild itself.

Chapter Eight

MAIDEN VOYAGE OF THE *TITANIC*

Titanic's maiden voyage, originally scheduled for 20 March, was announced. She would leave Southampton on 10 April 1912, right in the middle of a coal strike in Britain. Leaving Belfast on 2 April, her captain was E. J. Smith, making his last journey before retirement. She sailed directly to Southampton after basic sea trials, and work commenced in equipping her for a life of transatlantic service. Workers still swarmed aboard her, completing a snagging list of work, while stores were loaded onto her – everything from china and silverware to bottled beer, fine wines, and huge quantities of food. Coal was a big problem though and White Star scrambled round, trying to find enough Welsh steam coal to fill the 6,000 tons of bunkers aboard *Titanic*. Other ships' voyages were cancelled so *Titanic* could be coaled and she was opened to the public on Good Friday, with the monies collected going to seamens' charities. Dressed overall in flags, she was a magnificent sight. Behind the scenes, her crew was assembled, and she was readied for her first voyage to New York via Cherbourg and Queenstown. A change of First Officer would be made at Southampton and David Blair would leave, to be replaced by William Murdoch.

Towering above the Southampton skyline, as her sister had done proudly ten months before, *Titanic* was prepared for her maiden voyage. Work was still continuing aboard, and fresh flowers had been placed everywhere to mask the smells of paint that still permeated the ship. All around was a hive of activity as crew members rushed around in preparation for the throng that would descend on the ship through the course of the morning. Those crew not needed before today rushed to the ship before crew muster and stowed their bags away and got to work. The boilers were already being stoked and Thomas Andrews had boarded at 6 a.m. Many passengers had stayed over in the luxurious South Western Hotel, others in boarding houses around the dock area, but many were also coming from London in the two special boat trains that would leave Waterloo.

On the morning of the tenth, passengers began to arrive at the quayside, some had stayed the night before at the South Western Hotel, from where they could view the ship, while others travelled by special trains from London's Waterloo station. They were shown aboard to their cabins by the stewards and stewardesses, using the new-fangled electric lifts, and began to familiarise themselves with the ship and its myriad corridors and decks. Those in First Class saw the magnificence of the Grand Staircase, with its 'Honour and Glory' clock and glass dome above, while even those in Third Class were greeted by cabins and dormitories greatly superior to anything else afloat.

By twelve, the ship was ready and the ropes were let go. *Titanic* hauled her anchors up and, steam up, she sailed for New York with a complement of 324 First Class, 284 Second Class and 709 Third Class passengers, plus 891 crew. Crowds thronged the pier to say goodbye to loved ones, as passengers swarmed on deck to wave England goodbye for what would have been the last time for many of those who were emigrating. Already the ship was a veritable melting pot of cultures from Americans and British people to Scandinavians and the French.

At twelve, *Titanic* left berth 44. Tugs hauled her from the dockside and she nudged her way into the River Test. Because of the coal strike that had just finished, many steamers were berthed up and *Titanic* had to steam past the SS *New York*, an American Line ship, berthed next to the White Star's own *Oceanic* at berth 38. As *Titanic* put on speed, she came level to the *New York* and literally sucked her away from the side of *Oceanic*. *New York*'s mooring ropes snapped as if they were twine and only the quick thinking of the tug captains, especially of the *Vulcan*, saw disaster averted. The *New York* was nudged away from the *Titanic* just in time. *Titanic* was delayed as the *New York* was made secure. Soon she was on her way to Cherbourg and lunch was served, passengers being called by a bugler playing 'The Roast Beef of Old England'.

Loading passengers and mail in Cherbourg at dusk, the lights of *Titanic* blazed and she made a fine sight in the outer harbour.

Soon she would set sail for Queenstown, where she would arrive on Thursday morning. Passengers disembarked at Queenstown, including a Jesuit priest, Father Browne, whose photographs of his voyage would leave an enduring record of the short life of this magnificent ship. As well as people leaving, and mail being delivered to the ship's post office (over 1,300 sacks), passengers furiously completed final letters home. Most mail from Queenstown was stamped with a 3.45 p.m. Queenstown postmark, but some carried the ship's own special transatlantic post office postmark too.

The passengers soon settled into a routine of shipboard life. Those in First Class spent time in the palatial public rooms and in their large cabins. Some promenaded and others preferred the pleasure of their own private verandas. In Third Class, music from Irish pipes and violins could be heard. Some passengers read, others gossiped but all were impressed with this new queen of the sea.

The voyage, after the excitement of the *New York* incident, was passing quietly and quickly. It would all change dramatically on Sunday night. Warnings of ice had been coming in all day. The radio operators, Harold Bride and Jack Phillips, were receiving warnings as they also sent passengers' telegrams to friends ashore. Despite the warnings, extra boilers were being brought into service and speed was increasing. Sunday religious services had been performed, dinner had been served and passengers were relaxing or in bed when the inevitable happened and the ship, despite being in open ocean, hundreds of miles from land, steamed into a huge iceberg, puncturing her side. The Captain was quickly woken and the ship inspected. Soon, it was obvious she was doomed and Captain Smith ordered an SOS to be broadcast and the ship's boats prepared for launching. Few passengers believed the ship that 'as far as it is possible to do so … is designed to be unsinkable' was actually doomed, but she was. Within three hours, the then largest ship in the world would be gone, broken in two, with over 1,500 of her passengers and crew dead.

Many tales of heroism could be related of that fateful night, as well as tales of cowardice, but the characters that deserve special mention include the engineers who kept the ship's power going to the last, and who all died, the musicians who played almost to the end and the wireless operators who stayed at their posts till the batteries failed. As the final boats left the ship, it was obvious to those left that she was doomed. For one man, alone in front of the fire of the smoking room, a dream had died. Thomas Andrews, one of the visionaries who had created this magnificent ship, died aboard her a broken man.

This page, clockwise from top: Titanic *with steam up at Belfast prior to her sea trials. Below are three views of the ship at Southampton. Bottom left shows the stern of the* Titanic *but with the laid up mail steamers that had given their coal to the ship so she could make her maiden voyage. Both views below are by Southampton publisher Willsteed, who has snapped one side of the dock and then gone on moments later to photograph* Titanic *dressed overall in flags on the other side of the dock.*

White Star Royal Mail Steamer "Titanic".
Tonnage 45000 tons, Length 882½ feet, Breadth 92½ feet.

Above left: This postcard, issued by State Series of Liverpool, shows the *Titanic* at sea. Rather crudely drawn, it was issued pre-sinking and has even been seen postally used from on board the ship.

Above: This is one of the classic views of *Titanic*, photographed by Beken of Cowes as she left Southampton. The poop deck is awash with Third Class passengers.

Left: Titanic's port side at Berth 43 in the White Star Dock, Southampton.

Right: Titanic outward bound from Southampton.

Below, right: Captain Smith on the deck of *Olympic*.

Below: Southampton Docks Station was the arrival point of the special boat trains that left Waterloo Station on the morning of 10 April 1912. Some passengers had arrived the night before and stayed overnight in the opulent South Western Hotel.

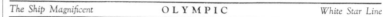

The Ship Magnificent   OLYMPIC   White Star Line

Above: A unique postcard of *Titanic*, snapped from the quayside. It shows the ship stern out, but with her bow still close to the deck. It matches closely the one directly below taken from the bow as her last rope is let go. The below view was photographed by G. Courtney and can be found in two versions, one pre- and one post-sinking.

Above, right: A view showing the boat deck of *Olympic*.

Below, right: The near miss of the SS *New York* and the *Titanic*.

Acres of deck space on this giant ocean liner (only two of the four funnels are shown above).

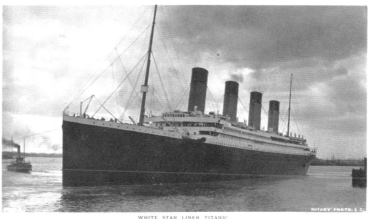

WHITE STAR LINER TITANIC
LENGTH 882 ft. 6 ins.   BREADTH 92 ft. 6 ins.   45,000 TONNAGE.
SAILED FROM SOUTHAMPTON ON HER ILL-FATED MAIDEN VOYAGE ON APRIL 10TH 1912 CARRYING 2,358 PASSENGERS AND CREW   STRUCK AN ICEBERG
OFF THE COAST OF NEWFOUNDLAND PERISHED ON MONDAY, APRIL 15TH 1912

This page: Three views of *Titanic* taken merely seconds apart, showing her turning out of the White Star Dock and into the main channel. The above view is by Courtney again, and also issued by the Nautical Photo Agency in the 1920s. Next to it is a view published by Rotary, a national postcard company that issued many postcards of important special events. Some are very rare and the author has a postcard of theirs showing the anchor chains of the Hamburg Amerika liner *Imperator* that has only ever surfaced a couple of times. Bottom, right shows *Titanic* photographed from the SS *New York*. The photographer next to the lifeboat has perhaps already got his snap. Was it one of the two above views?

This page: Two rare views (left) of *Titanic*. The first is by W. R. Hogg, of Ryde, who photographed *Titanic* from the end of Ryde Pier. Below shows her passing Cowes. The enterprising photographer has marked the King of Belgium's royal yacht, which was up for sale in 1912. Did he expect to get some sale of these cards to the new owners?

Above is a unique view taken from the dockside. *Titanic* is heading toward the line of cruisers we see on the Hogg image and the small bowsprit we see is that of the SS *New York*.

DEPARTURE AT LIVERPOOL, OF THE ILL-FATED S.S. "*Titanic*" OF THE WHITE STAR LINE WHICH SANK ON HER MAIDEN TRIP APRIL 15 TH 1912 WITH A LOSS OF OVER 1500 SOULS.

Above: There are many obvious errors with this postcard issued soon after the sinking. The postcard, at a rather jaunty angle, shows a German four-stacker at New York rather than the *Titanic*, which never once visited Liverpool. A famous American pair of cards used an image of the *Mauretania* to show the *Titanic* and *Carpathia* (with three funnels crudely removed). The lack of views of the brand new ship caused many problems for those wanting to cash in on the tragedy and many postcards issued show *Olympic*, which had been in service almost a year by the time *Titanic* was lost.

Above, right: *Titanic* at Cherbourg on the evening of 10 April 1912.

Below, right: Two tenders were based at Cherbourg. *Traffic* shown here was for Third Class passengers and luggage, while *Nomadic*, which still survives in Belfast, was for First and Second Class passengers.

CHERBOURG - Le " TRAFFIC " bateau transbordeur de la " White star Line " quitte la gare Maritime -

Edition Verschuere

Left and above, right: Titanic at Queenstown. These two views show Murdoch and Lightoller standing at the side of the ship viewing the tenders. The view to the right shows the White Star Wharf. On the 15th, the White Star flag would fly at half mast.

Below, right: Viewed from a passenger ship next to the ice floe, this is the scene that would have been seen on the evening of the 14th and in the morning of the 15th of April.

Above: Titanic firing distress rockets into the night.

Above, left: Another version of the card seen on the previous page. In this one, the publisher has managed to get the colour of the White Star burgee accurately in red. Behind is the cathedral of Queenstown.

Below, left: This postcard was published by an enterprising steward aboard the RMS *Carpathia*. He issued some fifty different views of the crew, passengers and of the rescue. The images were sold on to the American publisher Underwood & Underwood, who issued them as printed postcards. This is supposedly the iceberg which sank the *Titanic*.

Above: The passengers of the *Titanic* abandon ship.

Right: This view gives an idea of the scale of the iceberg...

This page: Views of the lifeboats. The above and bottom right views are artist's impressions, while the above, right view shows a lifeboat approaching the RMS *Carpathia*.

Above, left: Wireless played an important part in the loss of the *Titanic*. Positioned close enough to have rescued all of the passengers was the SS *Californian* of the Leyland Line. Her wireless operator had gone to sleep just before *Titanic* hit the iceberg. By the time she arrived on the scene, shown here, it was too late.

Below, left: The wireless room of the SS *Californian* in May 1914. The ship had only had radio installed in January 1912 and would be lost early in the First World War. This unique view shows Murphy at the key!

Above, right: *Mount Temple*, a Canadian Pacific Line ship, was also close enough to have resued the passengers but she lay, unmoving, all night.

Left: One of the heroes of the night was Harold Bride, shown here in his Junior Marconi Operator's uniform. After being rescued, he helped Harold Cottam on *Carpathia* to send the messages and survivor lists to Cape Race and New York.

Above, right: Lucille Duff Gordon, the dress designer.

Below, right: A series of views that appeared in the French magazine *L'Illustration*, but which were also issued by a Chicago company as a set of six postcards showing the sinking and splitting in two of *Titanic*.

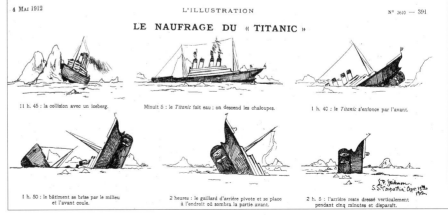

Chapter Nine

THE LIFEBOATS

Twenty lifeboats with a capacity of 1,178 persons were onboard the *Titanic*. Over 2,200 people were on the sinking ship and only 705 were rescued.

Much has been written about the *Titanic* disaster in the 100 years since the sinking and reference is being made even today whenever a shipwreck occurs, such as that of *Costa Concordia*. The main difference between modern shipwrecks and that of the *Titanic* is that a modern ship carries more than enough lifeboats to rescue every soul on board. It was one of the most far-reaching results of the disaster – lifeboats for all.

Titanic had lifeboat capacity for 52 per cent of those aboard, and less than 50 percent capacity if the ship was travelling full. This stemmed from a Board of Trade regulation that stated that ships over 10,000 tons must carry a minimum of sixteen lifeboats. These regulations were woefully out of date and, even at the time of disaster, moves were afoot to change the regulations although no decision had been made.

Alexander Carlisle, one of the driving forces of Harland & Wolff, had left the company to work with the Welin Davit Co.

and so Harland & Wolff were no strangers to the regulations concerning lifeboats. Despite the lack of lifeboat capacity, *Titanic* was within the law. A new davit type had been considered for the ship – one which would cope with forty-eight lifeboats – but it was decided to have only twenty lifeboats fitted, four above the legal minimum. This decision was to cost 1,500 lives. There is no doubt that had there been more lifeboats, almost all aboard the ship would have been rescued. The sea was calm, the ship sank on an even keel and it took over two hours for her to go down. Of course, *Titanic* was 'practically unsinkable', and this fallacy led to the lack of lifeboat provision.

The majority of the lifeboats themselves were constructed to a Board of Trade-approved design and had been designed by the chief draughtsman, Roderick Robert Crispin Chisholm, who was lost in the disaster as one of the nine-man Guarantee Group from Harland & Wolff. The lifeboats were of three different designs, with the majority being clinker-built wooden lifeboats, of 30 feet in length by 9 feet 1 inch breadth and 4 feet in depth from keel to rowlocks. These fourteen lifeboats were numbered evenly on the port side and odd numbers on starboard. They were grouped in two sets of four on each side. With elm keels and evenly spaced elm timbers, the stern and stem posts were built of oak and the boats clad in yellow pine, double fastened with copper nails (so they would not rust) then painted white. Each had copper buoyancy tanks and the seats were made of pitch pine. Around the gunwales were lifelines.

The ship itself was fitted with Welin davits of a new type, capable of launching three times, and the davit blocks were made of elm with lignum vitae roller sheaves, trebled for the ordinary lifeboats but just doubled for the smaller and lighter emergency cutters. Each lifeboat was equipped with a water beaker and provision tank and a sail, stored in a painted canvas bag, as well as all of the requisites demanded by the Board of Trade. These included blankets, provisions and flares, as well as a spirit boat compass and fitting, the compasses being stowed in lockers on the boat deck. Obviously, one of the things done before the lifeboat was launched was to fill the water tank and provision the lifeboat. Each of the fourteen lifeboats was capable of carrying sixty-five people and could be lowered from the boat deck full to capacity.

Two emergency cutters were fitted forward of the main lifeboats. These were always swung-out, ready for use at any time, and were meant to be used if someone fell overboard or a boat was needed to be sent off to another ship.

With a capacity of just forty persons, the emergency cutters were smaller than the standard lifeboats, with dimensions of 25 feet 2 inches x 7 feet 2 inches. Each was provisioned and supplied with a mast and sail. No. 1 was located on the starboard side and No. 2 on the port.

As well as these lifeboats, *Titanic* was fitted with four boats of an Engelhardt design. Captain Engelhardt, a Dane, designed the collapsible lifeboat at the turn of the twentieth century. It was designed to work as a raft, or, with its canvas sides up, as a lifeboat. In calm seas, it would float, laden with 4,000 kg, or the weight of forty people, with a 3–4 inch freeboard. Each was constructed of wood, with kapok (a kind of cork) as a buoyancy aid. The ones on *Titanic* had a capacity of forty-seven persons and were 27 feet 5 inches long by 8 feet breadth and 3 feet in height. Stowed upside down, they were intended to be launched from davits after the wooden lifeboats had been launched. They could be stored flat on the deck or against a bulkhead, thereby using relatively little deck space, which was the issue with the number of lifeboats on the boat deck and why their numbers had been cut from forty-eight, to thirty-two and then the paltry sixteen onboard when the ship sailed. Two of the Engelhardts were stowed on the roof of the officers' quarters, either side of the forward funnel and two stowed beside the emergency cutters.

The Engelhardts were robust, and three survived in the water to be rediscovered. Collapsible B was sunk with axes during the recovery of bodies, Collapsible A was found floating with three bodies in it a full month after the disaster, by the *Oceanic*, while one boat, possibly Collapsible C, was discovered nearly eighteen months afterwards, having floated for 1,800 miles almost to the entrance to the Caribbean. It was brought back to Avonmouth onboard an Elders & Fyffes ship.

Thirteen lifeboats were recovered by the *Carpathia*, and taken to New York, where they lay for a while, having been robbed of many items, including oars, nameplates and lifebelts left aboard. Seven were cast adrift, including all four collapsible boats, and three ordinary lifeboats. Four lifeboats were never seen again.

One of the failings of the officers on board the *Titanic* was not ensuring all of the boats left full. If they had, another 473 people would have been saved, total capacity being 1,178 persons, against 705 saved. This would have ensured every woman and child plus many men would have lived to tell their story. Some were sent down the falls part full as there were not enough people who were either in the vicinity or who would go in a lifeboat as they began to be launched. Those that opted to stay obviously decided the ship was not going to sink. Many boats were also launched partially full because the officers did not think they could be launched fully laden. All in all, it was a poor showing, and one that could have been resolved by ensuring the boats came back to the ship to be fully laden at a later point.

The disaster focused the mind of the Board of Trade and immediately after the sinking a huge number of lifeboats were constructed to fit aboard ocean liners. Nowadays, every ship carries enough lifeboats and life rafts for all crew and passengers, although the *Costa Concordia* sinking demonstrates clearly that there needs to be enough capacity even if lifeboats on one side are unusable due to listing.

Lifeboat launching sequence:

23.40: *Titanic* collides with iceberg
12.20: Lifeboats swung out
12.30: Women and children begin to be placed in lifeboats
12.45: Lifeboat No. 7 launched
12.55: Lifeboat No. 5 launched
12.55: Lifeboat No. 6 launched
01.00: Lifeboat No. 3 launched
01.00: Lifeboat No. 1 launched
01.10: Lifeboat No. 8 launched
01.20: Lifeboat No. 10 launched
01.20: Lifeboat No. 9 launched
01.25: Lifeboat No. 12 launched

01.30: Lifeboat No. 14 launched
01.30: Lifeboat No. 13 launched
01.35: Lifeboat No. 16 launched
01.35: Lifeboat No. 15 launched
01.40: Collapsible C launched
01.45: Lifeboat No. 2 launched
01.45: Lifeboat No. 11 launched
01.55: Lifeboat No. 4 launched
02.05: Collapsible D launched
02.20: Collapsible A floats off
02.20: Collapsible B washes off deck upside down
02.20 *Titanic* sinks

↓ 15 FEET FROM BOAT DECK TO WATER.

Left: Male passengers send their wives and sweethearts onto the lifeboats.

Above, right: Two lifeboats approach *Carpathia*. The first has had its mast up and is towing the collapsible behind.

Below, right: A J. W. Barker card showing one of the fifteen lifeboats that reached *Carpathia* approach.

"TITANIC" LIFEBOAT APPROACHING "CARPATHIA"
J. W. Barker, Copyright.

Left: A collapsible boat approaches *Carpathia*.

Below: Much propaganda was made of the lack of lifeboats for all.

Right: Another Barker view showing two lifeboats alongside *Carpathia*. While the first boat is quite full, the one behind is rather empty.

PUCK

LUXURIES VERSUS LIFEBOATS.

"TITANIC" LIFEBOAT ALONGSIDE "CARPATHIA"

J. W. Barker, Copyright.

Left: This view was published as the front page of the *Christian Herald*.

Below, left: This lifeboat could carry sixty or so people. Perhaps hundreds more could have been saved if only the boats had left full.

Right: Most of the lifeboats were brought aboard *Carpathia*, just in case...

HOISTING LIFEBOAT ABOARD "CARPATHIA".

J. W. Barker, Copyright.

Above, left: The lifeboats were dropped off in New York, where they remained for some time. Souvenir hunters stole many of the fixtures and fittings.

Above, right: A cartoon decrying the needless deaths of those in Second and Third Classes, who had less chance of survival.

Right: Found floating off Grand Cayman in 1913, this lifeboat was one of *Titanic*'s collapsibles. It is shown here aboard an Elders & Fyffes banana boat at Avonmouth, Bristol, upon the return of the ship to the UK. There are only two copies of this postcard known in the world.

Chapter Ten

THE AFTERMATH

Many changes took place after the loss of the *Titanic*. The most important were new regulations for lifeboat accommodation for all on board a ship, a new Ice Patrol in the North Atlantic and wireless manned at all times aboard passenger liners. For her sisters, *Olympic* and the *Britannic*, then under construction, the sinking would see much work done to both ships. For *Olympic*, she went to Belfast for an overhaul that involved fitting a double skin inside her hull that would see her set sail in April 1913, with the proclamation that she was 'two ships in one' and described as 'practically unsinkable' yet again.

Britannic would see her construction stopped until the results of the *Titanic* Inquiries in both the United Kingdom and United States were heard and she was launched in February 1914. War would see her fitting out delayed and she finally entered service as a hospital ship, making six journeys to Mudros in the Aegean. A mine saw the end of *Britannic* on 21 November 1916 and she now lies in around 400 feet of water off the island of Kea. She was the largest shipping loss of either world war and remains remarkably preserved to this day. One lucky crew member, Violet Jessop, had been aboard all three liners, having to abandon ship from two, and been on the third when it was rammed by HMS *Hawke*.

Today, thanks to the discovery of the *Titanic* in 1985, and the success of James Cameron's eponymous blockbuster film in 1997, she remains in the public viewpoint as the most famous shipwreck in history, a folly to Man's ambition and the power of nature. It seems as if the interest in *Titanic* will never cease.

TITANIC DISASTER APRIL 15TH 1912
1,635 PERISH AT SEA
① CAPTAIN SMITH. ② PHILLIPS, THE HERO OPERATOR.
3. RESCUING A PASSENGER. *Bonner, Arcade House, Whitley Bay.*

Left: One of many In Memorium postcards issued after the disaster. This one was published in Whitley Bay, England.

Right: Published by the National Series and pirated by numerous others, this postcard using the hymn 'Nearer My God to Thee' is one of the most common of all 1912 *Titanic* postcards.

Below, left: An American-published postcard with no details apart from what you see here. No mention of ship, or what disaster. It is part of a series of six issued by a Chicago publisher.

Below, right: A hand-made and unique stamp montage postcard posted soon after the disaster in France. With its element of hand-painting, this is truly folk art at its best.

Opposite: Olympic laid up after her crew mutined.

Wireless Operator Receiving Messages of Disaster

THE ILL-FATED WHITE STAR LINER "TITANIC."
LEAVING ON HER FIRST AND LAST VOYAGE. SUNK BY COLLISION WITH AN ICEBERG APRIL 15th, 1912, WITH
A LOSS OF 1,500 SOULS. THE GREATEST MARITIME DISASTER IN HISTORY.

Above: Numerous book post cards were issued of the *Olympic* and *Titanic*. This one is a rare view showing *Titanic* in the charge of four tugs in Belfast Lough.

Below: Another of the most common of the period *Titanic* postcards, this one shows Captain Smith and the ship. The view of the ship was also issued as a postcard too and is very common.

Below: Published in Guernsey, this, like many of the In Memorium cards issued in various parts of the UK, was in response to the outpouring of grief after the death of a local crew member or passenger. Bramley also published a cutaway view of *Titanic* too.

Above: Many postcards were issued abroad after the disaster, and not just in America or the UK. This one, still on sale in 1915, was published and posted in France.

Right: Published in Estonia, this In Memorium postcard was published and posted in Estonia. The view shown is actually of *Titanic*, rather than a view of *Olympic* adulterated. The author has cards published in Austria, Germany, Belgium, Italy, France and even in Russia in her collection.

Above: Three of the famous Bamforth-published postcards of the sinking. Available in both sepia and black and white printings, these are some of the most common postcards found in the UK of the disaster.

Above: The band of the Canadian liner *Royal George*, collecting funds outside the Bristol Seamen's Institute in April 1912.

Below: Awaiting news of the disaster at the White Star offices in New York.

Above: Survivors aboard the *Carpathia*.

Below: Memorial services were held all over the world, none more poignant than those in Halifax, where the bodies of the dead were recovered to.

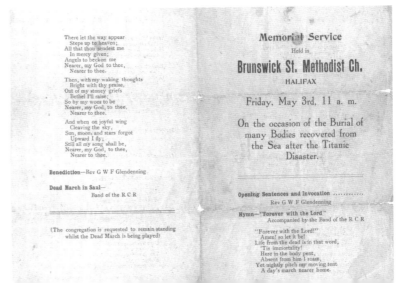

There let the way appear
Steps up to heaven;
All that thou sendest me
In mercy given;
Angels to beckon me
Nearer, my God to thee,
Nearer to thee.

Then, with my waking thoughts
Bright with thy praise,
Out of my stoney griefs
Bethel I'll raise;
So by my woes to be
Nearer, my God, to thee,
Nearer to thee.

And when on joyful wing
Cleaving the sky,
Sun, moon and stars forgot
Upward I fly;
Still all my song shall be,
Nearer, my God, to thee,
Nearer to thee.

Benediction—Rev G W F Glendenning

Dead March in Saul—
Band of the R C R

(The congregation is requested to remain standing whilst the Dead March is being played)

Memorial Service

Held in

Brunswick St. Methodist Ch.

HALIFAX

Friday, May 3rd, 11 a. m.

On the occasion of the Burial of many Bodies recovered from the Sea after the Titanic Disaster.

Opening Sentences and Invocation ....
Rev G W F Glendenning

Hymn—"Forever with the Lord"
Accompanied by the Band of the R C R

"Forever with the Lord!"
Amen! so let it be!
Life from the dead is in that word,
'Tis immortality!
Here in the body pent,
Absent from him I roam,
Yet nightly pitch my moving tent
A day's march nearer home.

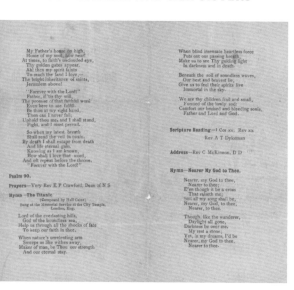

TITANIC MEMORIAL, SOUTHAMPTON 1914.

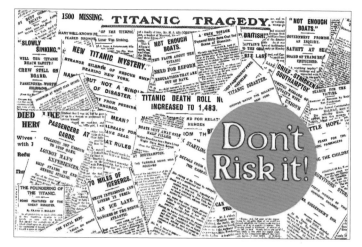

Above, left: The inside of the Memorial programme shown on the previous page.

Above, middle and right: This monument to the *Titanic* crew was unveiled in April 1914, on the second anniversary of the disaster. The middle view shows the wreath after the service, while the view above shows the unveiling. In some streets in Southampton, almost every adult male was lost.

Left: A 1913 advertising postcard used to convince travellers to take out insurance, using newspaper cuttings of the loss of the *Titanic*.

Above: The monument in Southampton is unveiled.

Below: A postcard of the Leeds musicians' memorial to the *Titanic* band. This painting still hangs in Leeds Art Gallery. Found in a cheap box of postcards.

Above: The biggest memorial to any crew member is this one in Godalming to Jack Phillips, the radio operator.

Below: The memorial in Southampton's The Avenue to the ship's firemen.

TITANIC MEMORIAL

Close-up views of just two of Southampton's *Titanic* memorials.

Left: An F. G. O. Stuart-published card of the Firemen's memorial.

Right: A private snapshot postcard of the Engineers' Memorial in Southampton. The Sixth Engineer, William Young Moyes, came from the author's home town. Like all of the engineers, he stayed at his post and tragically died.

MUSEUM GARDENS, LICHFIELD

Above, and right: Two views of the monument to Captain Edward Smith in Lichfield. Smith was born in Hanley, near Stoke on Trent but his memorial is at Lichfield, looking on to the Cathedral.

Far right: There are many memorials to the band of the *Titanic*, from the grave of Wallace Hartley in Colne to a bandstand in Broken Hill, Australia.

STATUE TO COMMANDER EDWARD JOHN SMITH, R.N.R.
RECREATION GROUNDS, LICHFIELD

HEROIC MUSICIANS OF THE TITANIC
who died at their posts like men ~ April 15th 1912

G. KRINS Violin.   W. HARTLEY BANDMASTER.   R. BRICOUX Cello

W. T. BRAILEY Piano   J. W. WOODWARD Cello

P. C. TAYLOR Piano

Nearer, my God, to Thee.

Or if on joyful wing cleaving the sky,
Sun, moon and stars forgot, upwards I fly,
Still all my song shall be,
Nearer, my GOD, to Thee, nearer to Thee.

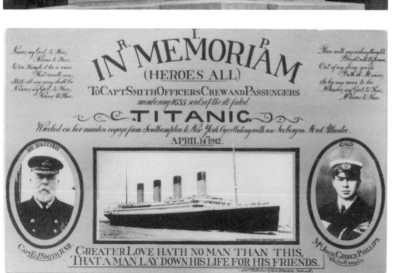

Above, left: The *Titanic* memorial on Liverpool's waterfront.

Above, right: Belfast's memorial is outside the city hall, on the left of the building if you are looking straight on. It was dedicated in 1920, and commemorates the 22 men from Belfast who died aboard the ship. A memorial hall to Thomas Andrews, the designer, is located in Comber, his home town.

Left: Published by E. A. Bragg of Falmouth, this card commemorates the 40+ Cornish crew and passenger victims of the *Titanic*, at least two of whom feature on postcards in this book.

Chapter Eleven

CARPATHIA – THE PLUCKY RESCUE SHIP

Designed to be an emigrant steamer, the single-funnelled *Carpathia* became famous when she rescued all the survivors of the *Titanic*. Her career was cut short by a German submarine in 1918.

It was a fine April morning in 1903 when the guests assembled at the Wallsend shipyard of Swan, Hunter & Wigham Richardson for the trial trip of their newest vessel. From the Tyne she would perform all the trials of a new vessel and then travel on to Liverpool, no longer in the ownership of her builders but now in the service of the Cunard Line. It was a proud time for Swan, Hunter, for they were tendering for the order to build a Cunarder a good twice the size of their new vessel, and one that would become just as famous. The former ship, a 13,555 grt vessel, was destined for the company's Mediterranean service to Boston and New York, the latter to be the fastest and largest ship yet built.

The smaller vessel was never designed to be a crack steamer and was capable of just 17 knots. Outward bound on her maiden voyage she averaged a mere 14.9 knots and on the return a slightly better 15.1 knots. What made the small emigrant steamer, with its single funnel, seven single-ended boilers, and quadruple expansion engines so important was a single event on an otherwise unimportant voyage from New York to Fiume in the Eastern Mediterranean.

There are not many people on this earth who have not heard of the events of that single night and there are few who have not seen the films, read the books, visited the exhibitions or seen references to it in newspapers, the internet or television. It was the night that made the *Carpathia*, for that was the name of the little steamer that sailed into history on that night to remember, and her captain, Arthur Henry Rostron, one of the most famous ships of all time. For, on that night in April 1912, Captain Rostron's command picked up a distress signal from the *Titanic*, then the world's largest man-made object. The *Titanic* was doomed, sinking quickly after ramming an iceberg in mid-Atlantic, some fifty-odd miles from the *Carpathia*. Captain Rostron urged a speed of 17 knots out of his vessel to reach the spot of the sinking as quickly as possible and managed to rescue 705 survivors.

But, what of the history of this plucky little vessel? Most of what has been written about *Carpathia* is of her part in the *Titanic* sinking but not so much of her life before and after the night of 14/15 April 1912. *Carpathia*'s keel was laid on 10 September 1901 and she was launched on 6 August 1902. She had accommodation for 400 saloon passengers, with a dining room for 200, spacious ladies' room, library and a gentlemen's smoking room. The prime trade for the *Carpathia* was to be the emigrant traffic from Austro-Hungary and its empire and Third Class could accommodate over 2,000 passengers in two-, four- and six-berth cabins. Like many Cunarders, she was designed to be converted in time of war to a troopship. The *Carpathia* could accommodate around 3,000 officers and men, plus 1,000 tons of stores. If carrying cavalry she could accommodate 1,000 officers and men, plus their horses, food and tack, and stores. She could also carry sufficient coal to steam for about 12,000 nautical miles at 15 knots, making her capable of steaming to the Cape of Good Hope or India.

The maiden voyage left from Liverpool on 3 May 1903, under the command of Captain Barr, destined for Boston. Punctually, at 11 a.m., the tender *Skirmisher* embarked over 1,000 Third Class passengers from all over Europe and at 3 p.m. the ship berthed at the Landing Stage. Loading of the many cases of luggage and the Saloon passengers began and by 4 p.m. the cry of 'All visitors ashore' was being made. Exactly fifteen minutes later the ropes were let loose and she began her maiden voyage. With a clear sky and smooth sea, she made her way down the Irish Sea for Queenstown. At 10 a.m. on the next day she was off Roches Point, Queenstown, and, as they boarded from the tender, the Irish emigrants were inspected by the doctor and then taken by white-coated stewards to their cabins. Meanwhile, members of the local press and Cunard's employees in Queenstown boarded the vessel to inspect it, along with hawkers selling bog oak, Irish laces and shawls. At 12.30 the tender sailed back to Queenstown with everyone not travelling to Boston.

For a few hours, the southern coast of Ireland was hugged until, slowly, land disappeared behind the ship, the last sighting of Europe being the Fastnet Lighthouse. On board were 145 saloon passengers, 1,741 third class and 244 crew, making 2,130. On 7 May 1903, a whisper went round the ship that there was an extra passenger aboard. The gossip was confirmed when an Irish woman was found to have given birth to a baby boy. On the morning of the 8th, a stiff breeze was encountered but the ship rode the heavy seas well. By the following Thursday she was berthed in Boston and the passengers disgorged. For the next two days, cargo was unloaded, with the last of the cargo, beef stowed in the refrigerated holds, being unloaded on the Saturday evening. As at Queenstown, on the Friday a delegation of Cunard agents visited the new ship. On the Sunday, 17 May, at 2 p.m. she left for Queenstown and Liverpool, arriving at the former on the 25th and the latter on 26 May.

Food consumed on the maiden voyage of the *Carpathia* is shown overleaf.

Tea	400 lb	Lamb	400 lb
Coffee	700 lb	Veal	100 lb
Sugar	3,700 lb	Pork	2,000 lb
Pickles	100 lb	Pig's heads	150 lb
Salt fish	1,500 lb	Ox liver	700 lb
Fresh fish	2,900 lb	Ox tails	90 lb
Fresh herrings	2,900 lb	Kidneys	160 lb
Mackeral	80 lb	Tripe	250 lb
Fresh beef	20,000 lb	Tongues	175 lb
Corned beef	350 lb	Sausages	160 lb
Mutton	3,340 lb	Jams and marmalades	850 lb

Cried fruit	700 lb		
Flour	100 barrels		
Ham	300 lb		
Bacon	1,250 lb		
Cheese	600 lb		
Eggs	8,000		
Butter	2,400 lb		
Potatoes	20 tons		
Ice cream	300 quarts		
Fresh milk	150 gallons		
Condensed milk	200 gallons		

For the next few years, *Carpathia* led an uneventful life, until 14/15 April 1912, when she rescued the surviving passengers from the *Titanic* and recovered thirteen of her lifeboats back to New York. On board on that voyage were numerous well-known people including the artist Colin Campbell Cooper and his wife Emma, as well as Charles H. Marshall, whose three nieces were travelling on the *Titanic*. On the morning of the 15th he was unexpectedly greeted by his nieces aboard *Carpathia*.

In 1914, James Bisset, Second Officer of *Carpathia*, noticed a group of Bosnian Serbs aboard the ship. It was only after 28 June 1914, and the assassination of Archduke Franz Ferdinand, that he realized the ship had carried the assassins.

At the start of the First World War, *Carpathia* remained in service but was also used to transfer American troops to France and Britain. On 17 July 1918, *Carpathia* departed in convoy from Liverpool and, two days later, was torpedoed three times by the submarine *U-55*. The first two torpedoes hit the port side and engine room, killing three trimmers and two firemen. *U-55* fired a third torpedo but was chased away by HMS *Snowdrop*, which picked up the fifty-five passengers and 218 surviving crew members. *Carpathia* sank about 120 miles from Fastnet.

On 9 September 1999, it was reported that the wreck of *Carpathia* had been found. She lay in 600 feet of water. However, this wreck turned out to be the Hamburg Amerika Line's SS *Isis*, which was lost in 1936. The next year, the real wreck of *Carpathia* was discovered, roughly where she had been reported sinking. Lying upright in 500 feet of water, the wreck has been mapped by RMS Titanic Inc., now known as Premier Exhibitions, and the ship's bell and numerous other items recovered.

Carpathia should have been a footnote in history, remembered by the families of those she carried to a new land, but became the most famous rescue ship of all time as a result of a few wireless messages, a dedicated Captain and a crew who obeyed orders and ensured she got to the site of the *Titanic*'s lifeboats as quickly as possible. Her captain at the time, Arthur Rostron, went on to become Commodore of the Cunard Line, while James Bisset, her Second Officer, also became a Cunard Line Commodore, captaining both *Queens*.

Above, left: Photographed on her outward bound voyage to New York in March 1912, the *Carpathia* is shown here at Valletta, Malta, on a postcard by J. W. Barker.

Above, right: Many Cunard postcards of this type do not name the ship, but this view is almost certainly of *Carpathia* at Palermo, Sicily.

Left: This view of Naples almost certainly shows *Saxonia* or *Ivernia*, near sister ships of *Carpathia*. Note the ventilation uptakes between the two forward masts.

Left: Crew members of the *Carpathia* aboard ship on her voyage previous to rescuing the passengers of the *Titanic*.

Right: A Cunard official postcard showing the promenade and boat decks of RMS *Carpathia*.

Below, left: Stewardesses aboard *Carpathia*. On the voyage back to New York they cared for the grieving *Titanic* passengers.

Left: A postcard issued by Cunard and, if you're lucky, adorning the top of a menu for the *Carpathia*, showing the ship leaving Messina.

Below, left: Dazed passengers from the *Titanic* congregate on the deck of the *Carpathia*.

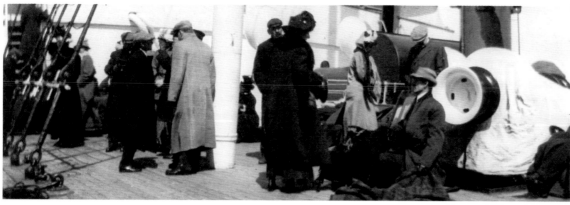

Left: Carpathia entering New York with the *Titanic*'s survivors aboard.

Below, left: With shell doors open, *Carpathia* is shown in Liverpool *c.* 1903.

Right: Berthed at New York, *Carpathia* would discharge the survivors at the White Star Pier before resuming her voyage to Europe.

Chapter Twelve

BRITANNIC – DAMNED BY DESTINY

The ill-fated sister to *Titanic* and *Olympic*, and the largest shipping loss of either world war, RMS *Britannic* is often forgotten, despite the interest in her two older sisters.

Three White Star Line vessels have held the name *Britannic*. The first and third both had long and successful careers, but the second *Britannic*, the third *Olympic*-class ship, was never to carry a fare-paying passenger, nor ever make a transatlantic voyage.

The first *Britannic* was built in 1874 and was to remain in company service for almost thirty years and captured the Blue Riband in 1876 at an average speed of 16 knots. Originally to be named *Hellenic*, she was renamed on the stocks. Her sister *Germanic* was to have an even longer career, being sold to a Turkish company and not being scrapped until 1950, having been in service for seventy-five years.

The second *Britannic* was a rather more special ship and would hold numerous records, some to be proud of, while others marked her down as a failure for her owners. She would be fitted with the world's largest ever reciprocating steam engines, she would never carry a fare-paying passenger, nor would she

ever reach New York. *Britannic* was also to become the First World War's largest shipping loss, something that even the loss of the *Empress of Britain* in the Second World War would not surpass. This truly magnificent vessel would sail on only six voyages, all to the Mediterranean, before she succumbed to a mine laid by a German submarine operating out of Pola in the Adriatic. She was the second 'unsinkable' ship to sink after meeting disaster, despite a redesign of her hull to accommodate a second skin that was intended to prevent the same sort of fate that met *Titanic*.

Britannic was almost an afterthought, the third of three White Star leviathans designed to operate a weekly service between Southampton and New York with her sisters *Olympic* and *Titanic*. There is even confusion about her original name, with some orders, such as that with Noah Hingley, of Cradley Heath, for her anchor (the largest ever made), listing her as No. 433 *Gigantic*. The name was supposedly changed after the loss of her sister in 1912. Her two sisters had been built side by side at Queen's Island in Harland & Wolff's Belfast yard, with *Olympic* entering service in June 1911 and *Titanic* in April 1912. Once *Olympic* was launched, her slipway was cleared ready to take the new leviathan, which was given the build number 433.

Work was well underway with *Britannic* when *Titanic* hit an iceberg. Her keel had been laid on 30 November 1911 on the slip that *Olympic* had vacated a year earlier, when she was launched on 20 October 1910. Work ceased almost immediately on Hull No. 433 as the outcome of the two enquiries into *Titanic*'s loss showed that the system of watertight bulkheads had failed due to poor design, causing a domino effect that pulled the ship deeper and deeper into the icy cold Atlantic. Thomas Andrews, the designer of the three ships, who had sailed as part of Harland & Wolff's guarantee group, and who had been making copious notes on how to improve the third of the class, had also died in the sinking and his tragic death also created huge problems for the Belfast yard.

Gigantic saw her name changed rather quickly to *Britannic*, and a redesign was made to her hull. The double bottom was deepened from 5 feet to 6 feet and a double skin extended well above the waterline. Weak areas of the hull were strengthened too. Huge lifeboat davits of a new design that could each launch as many lifeboats as could be fitted to the ship, and that swung the boats so far out from the side of the ship that they could be launched even when the ship had a list, were installed too, all to give the illusion that *Britannic* was a hugely-improved, and much safer, bigger sister of *Titanic*.

Work progressed slowly, not only due to the redesign but also because the loss of *Titanic*, and near loss and subsequent loss of revenue after *Olympic*'s collision with HMS *Hawke* in September 1911. Sometime before November 1911, her breadth was changed

so she would be 18 inches wider than her sisters. War was also looming as *Britannic* neared completion. She was launched at the end of February 1914, into an uncertain future. White Star themselves announced an entry into service in spring 1915 and the publicity machine began to extol the virtues of the newest addition to the company's fleet. She was not even the largest ship afloat when she was launched as that honour had already passed to Hamburg Amerika's *Imperator*, but White Star would ensure she was the most luxurious, as *Olympic* and *Titanic* had been before her. Her First Class accommodation was the first to offer toilets in almost every cabin, with only the most basic of First Class cabins on D and E Decks having to use communal facilities.

Already, by February 1914, Britain was preparing for war and ship-building materials were being diverted to ships of war and cargo shipping, with little being available to complete *Britannic*. Gradually, as spring turned into summer, workmen were diverted to more pressing vessels. In August 1914, war was declared and work ceased. Many of the interior spaces of *Britannic* were unfinished and, despite rumours that the war would be over by Christmas, it rumbled on and on. The Western Front had become bogged down, literally, and the war had become a global conflict. German and Austro-Hungarian ally Turkey was set to enter the war. The narrow straits of the Dardanelles would prevent supply of the Russian armies in the Black Sea area and it was decided to invade them and seize control. On 25 April 1915, British, Empire and French troops landed at Gallipoli. It was the start of an ill-fated campaign that would see the deaths of over 70,000 Allied and 20,000 Turkish soldiers. Casualty rates were horrendous, as the Allies were tied down on the beaches, with little hope of defeating the Turks. This was just one of four fronts the Ottoman Turks were fighting on and casualties were huge. It meant that some of the biggest liners in the world were needed as troopships and hospital ships.

After a few months of toing and froing between White Star and the Admiralty, *Britannic* was requisitioned on 13 November 1915. Work began in earnest to fit her out as a hospital ship. Her empty decks now thronged with workmen, all rushing to complete her. Medical supplies were ordered, her public rooms were fitted out as wards and operating theatres, much of the fixtures and fittings intended for her were placed into storage for the duration and she was painted an all-over white, with green stripe and three huge red crosses along her sides, and other red crosses that could be lit at night on her promenade deck. Only five of the revolutionary new lifeboat davits had been fitted and standard Welin davits were hurriedly added to bring her lifeboat complement up to fifty-five. Stacks of Linkleter floats were arranged anywhere there was space on the boat deck. She would, after all, be capable of carrying a crew, doctors and nurses and wounded soldiers and would need capacity for 4,473 people, representing 3,309 casualties, 675 crew and 489 medical staff.

On the evening of 11 December 1915, *Britannic* sailed from Belfast for Liverpool, where, ten days later, provisioned and staffed, she set sail on her maiden voyage to Naples. Her captain would be Charles Bartlett, who had overseen construction of the *Titanic* and *Britannic*. Arriving in Naples on 28 December 1915, she was coaled and sailed for Mudros, where she got up to full speed for the first time. With more powerful engines, she was slightly faster than her sisters, with a top speed of 24 knots.

Arriving at Mudros on New Year's Day, the job of transferring over 3,300 patients to her began. They came from Gallipoli in smaller hospital ships and were loaded aboard *Britannic*, which sailed for England on 3 January, arriving at Southampton for the first time on 9 January.

After unloading her passengers into waiting hospital trains, which took them all over southern England, and even Wales, she was provisioned again and prepared for her next voyage, which commenced on 20 January 1916. Instead of sailing for Mudros, this time she remained in Naples and loaded about 2,200 sick and wounded there, leaving on 4 February. The campaign in the Dardanelles settled down and there was little need for such a large ship on the service, so *Britannic* was laid up in Southampton until mid-March. On the 20th, she sailed again for Naples, coaling there then proceeding to Augusta, where the injured were transferred to her and she set sail for Southampton again, completing her third successful voyage on 4 April 1916.

Laid up off Cowes after her third voyage, *Britannic* was released back to White Star on 6 June. But, barely eleven weeks after her return to Belfast, she was called back up again on 28 August 1916. The reasons for the lowering of numbers of casualties from February was the evacuation of the Dardanelles after the aborted invasion, but the Salonika front opened up after the Bulgarians entered the war. Casualty numbers were huge and the big hospital ships were required again. Captain Bartlett again took command and took the *Britannic* to Cowes. For a fortnight preparations took place for her next voyage. Outward bound she carried Voluntary Aid Detachment nurses and medical supplies. Setting sail on 24 September 1916, she was once more en route to Naples. On 1 October, she made the voyage to Mudros, which was the Allied base in the Aegean. Arriving there on the 3rd, she loaded over 3,300 wounded soldiers, leaving again on the 5th. By the 11th, she was back in Southampton unloading the soldiers onto waiting hospital trains.

On the 13th, the Royal Army Medical Corp requested that *Britannic* be used to transfer personnel and supplies to the front yet again. On the 20th, *Britannic* was ready to sail. In five days, she was in Naples, where she remained for a day and a half. Arriving in Mudros on 28 October, the task of loading her passengers began again. Distributed into wards depending on their injuries, some men were walking wounded and could wander the ship. The fully-functioning hospital was well used but the carrying of an Austrian wounded soldier would create huge problems for the British Government. Adalbert Messany was ill with tuberculosis and, despite being a prisoner since the start of the war, the decision had been made to repatriate him.

Messany was aboard *Britannic* as she was still unloading her medical supplies and RAMC personnel, all in khaki uniform, and wrongly assumed they were British soldiers, which *Britannic* could not, under international law, carry. Messany also noted that some of the British wounded still carried sidearms, again a breach of the Geneva Convention. On 30 October, *Britannic* sailed for home, her crew and passengers unaware of the diplomatic incident that would engulf the British in January 1917, after Messany had returned to Austria.

Of course, by then *Britannic* would be gone, sunk in the Aegean, thankfully without a cargo of wounded. Completing her penultimate voyage on 6 November, she was prepared again for what would be her final voyage. On her final voyage was Violet Jessop, who had been a stewardess aboard *Olympic* when she was rammed by the *Hawke*, was rescued from *Titanic* as she sank and was now on the last of the *Olympic*-class vessels as a VAD nurse. HMHS *Aquitania* had been damaged in a storm and, so, *Britannic* was readied in record time for her next voyage to Mudros. It took six days to prepare her and she sailed once more on 12 November.

With no passengers, the medical staff had the run of the ship and on 17 November the vessel was in Naples once more. A huge storm delayed departure and *Britannic* finally left Naples late on the 18th. On Tuesday, 21 November 1916, *Britannic* was in the Aegean, less than a day from Mudros and the hectic loading of wounded soldiers. It was 8 a.m. and the medical staff were enjoying breakfast as the ship cruised at 20 knots. At 8.12, a roar was heard and the ship shook, shuddering as if she had hit something. A huge hole had appeared between cargo holds 2 and 3 and the ship began to take on huge quantities of water. There had been no wake from a torpedo and *Britannic* was a hospital ship so no U-boat captain would have dared try to sink her. What had happened? *Britannic* had been mined! An indiscriminate mine left by a U-boat out of Pola had been the death of White Star's finest vessel.

But *Britannic* had seen many safety features built into her as a result of the sinking of her sister, *Titanic*, so what had happened to cause her to sink? It seems that, as the mine had struck so close to a shift change, watertight doors were still open. From the forepeak to cargo hold 3, the water was pouring in and the damage had caused *Britannic*'s watertight doors to jam open. Also, against regulations, many portholes were open in the heat and with six watertight compartments letting in water, the ship was ultimately doomed. An SOS was sent, with HMS *Scourge* responding within three minutes of the collision. *Britannic* was already settling heavily by the bow and it was obvious she had not long to live. As other ships began to sail to her aid, Bartlett ordered the lifeboats ready for launching, while simultaneously trying to sail *Britannic* for the shallow shores of the island of Kea. The island was a mere two miles away and the engines were brought up to full speed, but the result of this vain effort to save the ship was to fill her more rapidly with water. Fifteen minutes after the explosion, *Britannic*'s bow was almost under water and she was listing badly to starboard. Her E-deck portholes were now submerged, despite once being 20 feet above the waterline. Water poured through the open portholes as the crew and medical staff prepared to abandon ship.

She was still underway as the first boats hit the water and one boat was dragged into the still-turning port-side propeller. It churned up the lifeboat, turning it into matchwood, while causing horrific injuries to the poor passengers. A second lifeboat met the same fate, luckily all aboard except for Violet Jessop, jumping into the water well before the churning propeller. She jumped into the water and was dragged down, rising to the surface and fracturing her skull on a piece of floating wreckage. She floated in a sea of red, with severed limbs and smashed timbers. A third boat had a lucky escape as Bartlett ordered the engines stopped, the crew being able to push themselves clear of the bronze blades. One of the new davits failed to work but the others proved their worth as the remaining passengers and crew left the ship. At nine o'clock, the last lifeboat left the ship. Twenty-eight had left, along with the two motorboats, and the captain and officers jumped off the starboard bridge wing as it reached the water. A couple

of stragglers left just after this, and Bartlett floated in the water watching his command sink in front of him. In a depth of only 400 feet of water, the ship's bow struck the soft and she pirouetted round as she settled. Her funnels collapsed as she rolled onto her starboard side. Fifty-five minutes after being mortally wounded, *Britannic* was gone forever. The largest shipping loss of either world war had gone to the bottom, thankfully with the loss of a mere thirty fatalities. Of those on board, 1,032 were saved, with the motorboats being used to pick up those floating in the warm waters off Kea. On her sixth voyage, *Britannic* was no more. She was never to serve on the three-ship, weekly transatlantic service envisaged by Bruce Ismay and Lord Pirrie back in 1907, nor would she ever sail to New York. Instead, *Britannic* has spent much of the past ninety-seven years as a footnote to the history of *Titanic* and *Olympic*.

Discovered again in the 1970s by Jacques Cousteau, the wreck of *Britannic* is in excellent condition and is now owned by the author Simon Mills. There have been plans to turn her into an underwater museum, but for now she remains in 400 feet of crystal-clear water, a reminder of the futility of war. Thankfully, her death saw only thirty casualties and if she had hit the mine on the return voyage, the story would have been much more tragic, with the loss of hundreds, if not thousands, of wounded soldiers, skilled nurses and doctors and crew. Had she survived, she would have been one of the most luxurious ships afloat for much of the 1920s. Instead, some of her fittings went to *Olympic* during her 1919 refit, while yet others were sold off, some surviving in a Belfast pub. Nowadays, all that remains are a few wooden panels, some furniture and the majestic wreck.

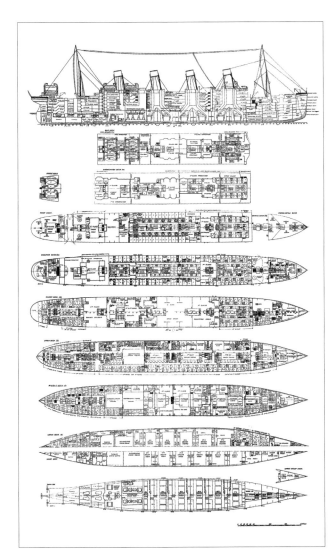

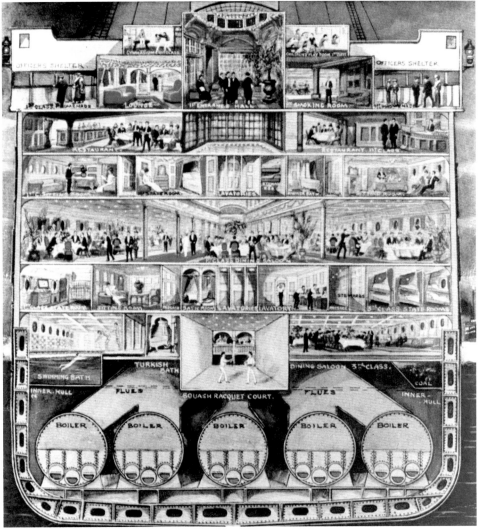

Three views by Robert Welch of construction work on the *Britannic*, Harland & Wolff's Yard No. 433.

Left: Looking down from the Great Gantry onto a plated *Britannic*. There is a wealth of detail here, from the holes for the cargo holds to the machine rivetters visible next to the funnel openings.

Above, right: In Harland & Wolff's machine shop are just some of the boilers for No. 433.

Below, right: The keel and double bottom of *Britannic* are laid. Soon ribs will reach skyward, ready to be plated.

Above: Few postcards exist showing *Britannic* in her company livery. This one, by F. G. O. Stuart, of Southampton, is one of the rarest.

Below: A company issued postcard, one of a set of three, showing *Britannic* ready for launching in February 1914.

Above: Taken from a passing steamer, this rather dark view shows *Britannic* almost ready for launching.

Below: Published by Hurst, of Belfast, this view is the real photo version of the card next to it.

Launch of a Giant Liner. Belfast. (7)

Above, left: The *Britannic* was fitted with the world's largest reciprocating engines. These powered the outer propeller shafts. The steam from these was exhausted into a low pressure turbine, shown here in the engine shop at Harland & Wolff. The man to the right gives an idea of scale.

Above, right: Issued by the White Star Line soon after the launch, this view shows *Britannic* in her company livery, along with the lifeboat davits that would distinguish her from her two sisters.

Left: Simply captioned 'Launch of a Giant Liner, Belfast', this is *Britannic* entering the water.

Above: Harland & Wolff's floating crane loads a boiler aboard *Britannic*.

Below: Published in France, this view shows *Olympic*, but is captioned *Britannic*.

Above: The *Britannic* never entered company service, being requisitioned as a hospital ship. She is here, probably in January 1916, being coaled in Southampton. A machine coaler is by her side, a great advance on hand coaling.

Below: Sold on board, this view shows *Britannic* in her hospital ship livery.

This page: Four views of *Britannic* as a hospital ship.

Above: Printed by Sanbride, a company from Middlesbrough, this view was sold aboard ship to wounded soldiers returning home.

Below: *Britannic* in Southampton Water. She would return to Southampton and smaller vessels would take the wounded to Netley, or she would be discharged into waiting hospital trains for onward travel to hospitals throughout the UK.

Above: At Mudros, with HMS *Nelson* and HMS *Triad*. This is one of the last ever views of *Britannic* above water.

Below: W. E. Axten of Southampton published many views of hospital ships. This is the original artwork for a postcard of *Britannic*. Done on thin card, the image itself is identical in size to the completed postcard and still shows signs of the original pencil drawing under the pen and ink sketch.

Chapter Thirteen

OLYMPIC – THE OLD RELIABLE

After a major refit in late 1912, the *Olympic* re-entered service in April 1913, with a new double skin and two furnaces converted for oil-burning. Her passenger accommodation had been slightly re-worked and her new tonnage became 46,358 as a result of the work. White Star advertised her as the all-new *Olympic*, proclaiming her practically unsinkable yet again, due to the new double skin and reworked watertight compartments that would ensure no repeat of the loss of *Titanic*. For the next two years she sailed back and forth across the Atlantic, but in August 1914 the culmination of years of arms race and political shenanigans in Europe had led the continent to war. The conflict saw *Olympic* keep to her Atlantic schedule, despite the threat from U-boats, but in October 1914 that was all to change as she firmly became involved in the war.

However, as an aside, right at the beginning of the war, the German liner *Kronprinzessin Cecile*, outward bound from New York, was in danger of being captured by the British. At sea when war was declared, she turned back and headed for the US again. Her captain had the funnel tops painted black, so that with a buff and black colour scheme, she may be mistaken at

a distance for the *Olympic*. Berthed at Bar Harbor, Maine, she confused the locals, who were surprised to see the '*Olympic*' in the bay. Meanwhile, the navy was furious at losing the *Cecile*, which was interred for the duration.

Twice *Olympic* sailed from Liverpool to New York, and on 26 September 1914, she visited the Clyde, the largest White Star vessel ever to sail there. It was decided to lay her up after her return voyage from New York on 21 October 1914, and so *Olympic* sailed for Liverpool once again, with her smallest complement of passengers – a mere 153. The northern approaches to Liverpool had been mined by the converted liner *Berlin* and it was one of those mines that would see *Olympic* attempt to tow one of Britain's largest and newest battleships, the 1912 HMS *Audacious*, to safety after she had been hit by a mine off the Irish coast on 27 October 1914. *Olympic* was perhaps ten miles away and answered the distress call. With a heavy sea running, the lifeboats were launched from *Olympic*'s starboard side and they made their way to the sinking *Audacious*, hauling off many of her crew. 450 were delivered to the navy ships around the stricken vessel and 250 onto *Olympic* herself. Around

200 remained to help save the ship. A cable was transferred from *Olympic* and attempts were made to tow *Audacious* into Lough Swilly. The cable broke and it was obvious that *Audacious* was doomed. Abandoned, at 9.00 pm, almost twelve hours after she hit the mine, an explosion ripped her apart.

For a week *Olympic* was detained in Lough Swilly, before going to Belfast on 3 November 1914. The passengers and crew were sworn to secrecy over the sinking – the navy did not want the Germans to know of the loss of a crack battleship. However, with so many passengers aboard, the truth did come out, and even the attempts to create a dummy battleship using the Canadian Pacific's *Montcalm* failed. *Olympic* was laid up until 1915, when she was called up as a troopship.

A new front was opening in the Dardanelles and British and Empire troops were required in huge quantities to fight the Turks. In September 1915, after months of discussion, *Olympic* was requisitioned. With accommodation for 6,000 troops, and guns, including a 12-pounder fitted, she sailed on 25 September 1915 from Liverpool. The ship rescued the survivors of the French vessel *Provincia* on 1 October, off Mudros, and she fired at a submarine later that day. Two further submarine attacks in 1916 followed.

In March 1916, after four voyages to Mudros, she was transferred to the Halifax run, to bring Canadian troops to Britain. She soon became known as 'Old Reliable' as she sailed back and forth with troops. In November 1916, her sister *Britannic*, converted to a hospital ship, was lost to a mine in the Aegean. Soon after, in 1917, Olympic was refitted and overhauled, 6-inch guns were installed and she was painted in a dazzle paint scheme, seen on one of the most famous views of her, taken from the air by a British seaplane.

On 12 May 1918, *Olympic* would make history again. She had been shadowed by the submarine *U-103* and, spotting the German submarine, she turned and fired a gun at it. It missed, but *Olympic* was on collision course. Her commander, Bertram Hayes, ordered her hard a port and the *Olympic* smashed into the *U-103* close to her conning tower. The sub surfaced, mortally damaged, and most of her crew were rescued by the USS *Davis* as the *U-103* slipped beneath the waves forever.

At the end of the war, *Olympic* made many voyages repatriating Canadian troops and in February 1919 she returned to Belfast. Upon dry-docking, it was found that she had a dent in her hull amidships – caused by a torpedo that had failed to explode. She had had a lucky escape. In Liverpool on 21 June 1919, *Olympic*, one time Ship Magnificent and now simply known as Old Reliable, completed her trooping service and was returned to White Star, having carried around 200,000 passengers and soldiers in wartime. She sailed for Belfast and months of work to refit her for passenger service, with her owners safe in the knowledge that she had made a major contribution to the war, having carried one in six of all Canadian troops to or from the conflict, having sunk a submarine, and been the most successful of all of the superliners in a time of crisis. Her refit had been hard earned and was badly needed.

Right: Issued by the White Star Line, this view shows *Olympic* in New York just prior to the First World War.

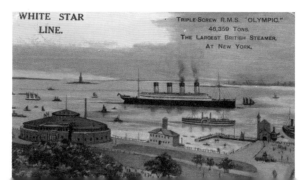

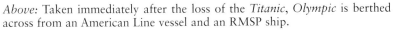
THE WHITE STAR DOCK, SOUTHAMPTON.

Above: Taken immediately after the loss of the *Titanic*, *Olympic* is berthed across from an American Line vessel and an RMSP ship.

Below: Published by an unknown publisher, this view shows the Dining Saloon aboard ship. It was issued in the 1920s.

Gymnasium, R.M.S. "Olympic."

Above: The gymnasium aboard *Olympic*. One of these Georgian-style windows was purchased by the author in Haltwhistle, where many fittings from *Olympic* went when she was scrapped.

Below: *Olympic* took part in the rescue of the crew of HMS *Audacious*, sunk in October 1914 by German mines.

The Sinking of H.M.S. "Audacious" in the Irish Sea, by a German Mine, during the Great War - 1914.

Above: With her lifeboats in the water, *Olympic* stands by to rescue the crew of HMS *Audacious*.

Below: After taking part in the rescue, *Olympic* sailed for the Clyde, where she is shown with the Caledonian Steam Packet Company's paddle steamer *Duchess of Fife*, which tendered her and took the passengers to Greenock for onward travel.

Above: British army and navy reservists are waved to by crew of the *Olympic* in New York harbor, as they return back to Britain at the beginning of the war.

Below: Laid up on the Clyde in 1916, the *Olympic* spent some time here along with *Mauretania* at the end of the Gallipoli campaign.

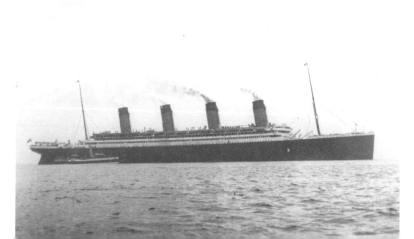

Above: Another view of *Olympic* in 1916 on the Clyde. Wartime views from non-official sources are very hard to find as photography was effectively banned.

Above: The largest British liners would only travel to Mudros, and smaller ships would take troops onwards to the Dardanelles. HMT *Olympic* is here at Mudros; note the guns at her bow.

Below: From late 1916, *Olympic* trooped to Canada and back. This view shows her at Halifax, Nova Scotia.

Below: Canadian troops aboard HMT *Olympic* on one of her many transatlantic wartime crossings.

Left: A postcard view of *Olympic* in dazzle paint published by G. A. Pratt. Pratt was a female maritime bookseller and postcard publisher in Southampton.

Right: Photographed from 800 ft by a seaplane from the seaplane base at Portland, Dorset, this view shows *Olympic* steaming hard up the English Channel in 1918.

Left: Olympic from 1,000 feet, stopped in the Solent.

Middle, left: With her destroyer screen, *Olympic* returns to Southampton with some 3,000 Canadian soldiers aboard.

Below, left: These cards were issued to members of the Canadian Expeditionary Force as they reteturned back to Canada at the end of the war.

Right: The classic company-issued postcard of *Olympic* photographed from a seaplane. Based on a photograph and colourised at the time, this image also appears on a superb poster, as well as in black and white. Note the 6-inch guns at the stern and the thousands of troops on her decks.

Chapter Fourteen

THE POST-WAR YEARS OF *OLYMPIC*

In October 1919, the *Olympic* was again in Belfast, this time not a troopship, but as a passenger liner once more. Harland & Wolff were refitting her for civilian service again, and they worked from stem to stern and from keel plate to mast-top to refurbish her. The most major change to her would be the conversion of her boilers to oil-firing. A trial had been undertaken pre-war with two of her boilers and, despite the extra price of oil over coal, the benefits of a much reduced engineering staff, as well as cleaner, faster turnarounds were simply too great.

As well as new boilers, much work was undertaken on the turbines, new fireproof doors were added on every deck, the plumbing and wiring were overhauled and the passenger accommodations refitted. Many items that had been in storage during the war were returned to Belfast and fitted to the ship, while some of the brand new fixtures and fittings no longer need for her sunken sister *Britannic* were also sent aboard. Lifeboats were replaced and their configuration changed, to accommodate extra boats. Carpets were replaced, especially in the passenger cabins, which saw linoleum widely used throughout the ship.

On 17 June 1920, *Olympic* set sail for Southampton and for a new, exciting period of her career. 4,000 men had been involved in the refit of the first oil-burning superliner. At noon, on Friday 25 June 1920, with 2,249 passengers aboard, *Olympic* set sail for New York. She would soon prove herself to be one of the most popular ships afloat.

Olympic was not to have the benefits of her sisters as running mates, making do with smaller ships such as *Adriatic*, but she would soon have a worthy running mate in the ex-*Bismarck*, a Hamburg Amerika liner, which had been under construction at the war's start and had been sold to White Star as war reparation for the loss of *Britannic*, the largest ship built in the United Kingdom to date. Cunard and White Star had agreed between themselves to buy the *Imperator* and *Bismarck*, renaming them *Berengaria* and *Majestic* respectively, while the third HAPAG ship went to the United States Line as *Leviathan*.

In October 1924, *Olympic*'s finest moment would be when she carried Edward, Prince of Wales. She was already a choice of film stars, business men and millionaires, but she could now add royal patronage too. The Prince, who would become infamous as the King who abdicated, and his entourage, took a Parlour Suite.

Another collision in March 1924 would confirm the danger of collision. *Olympic*, when leaving New York, was rammed by the *Fort St George*, a Furness Bermuda liner. Initially, it looked as if *Olympic* had escaped relatively unscathed but her stern post had been fractured. In 1925, it was replaced; the first time such a major undertaking had been performed on such a large vessel. In December 1927, *Olympic* was refitted once again, this time concentrating on the ship's accommodation. The most major change, and one that would affect many passengers in First Class, was that she was retrofitted with toilets in many First Class cabins. New suites were added, and many others redecorated. A new Tourist Class was introduced, with the company hoping to capitalise on those Americans who wanted to return to the Old World to visit.

The new stern post caused some concern though, with pitting of the post around the aperture for the central propeller. This was worked on, with white metal used as a sheath over this area. On 18 November 1929, soon after the Wall Street Crash, *Olympic* was shaken and shuddered for a whole two minutes. No evidence of damage was found and it was assumed, correctly, that she was over the site of an underwater earthquake. It severed over half of the transatlantic cables and *Olympic*'s position at the time was useful in working out where the breaks were.

By 1931, *Olympic*'s hull was twenty years old and she was showing signs of wear and tear. The Board of Trade inspectors noted that cracks were evident in the ship's structure. They were welded or plated over but a more careful inspection was made

of the ship from then on. For 1931, she was issued with a six-monthly passenger certificate, which was updated in August. Times were hard and *Olympic* was sent cruising out of New York in 1931. This had advantages for both White Star and the predominantly American passengers. Prohibition saw the closure of legal bars in the USA and a ban on imports of alcohol, but outside the territorial waters the bars on European vessels would be flung open and passengers could, if they so desired, drink themselves silly. *Olympic* cruised to Halifax, Nova Scotia, in August, with many ex-soldiers aboard her during this time.

In the winter of 1932, *Olympic* would have her last large refit, with work concentrating on the engines. Entering service in 1933, she was like a new vessel once more. Her engines were running superbly and her passenger accommodation had been titivated. The passenger areas had seen a makeover and many areas of once-beautiful wood paneling had been repainted in green or white. All this, despite White Star running at a loss. 1934 would see major changes afoot as White Star and Cunard were forced to merge by the government. Both lines needed subsidies to survive but the government could not pay for both, especially as passenger trade was down. An Act of Parliament saw the two companies merge, the government lend money to Cunard White Star for the completion of Hull 534, which would become the *Queen Mary*, and a sister ship, as yet un-named.

The merger created a challenge in that the merged line had too many ships, especially crack liners, most of which were also over twenty years old. It was decided that *Mauretania*, the speed Queen of the Atlantic, and *Olympic* would be the big ships to go and both would be retired from service by 1935, *Mauretania* being first to go, her last voyage taking place as the

Queen Mary was launched. In May of 1934, however, *Olympic* would be involved in another collision, this time in thick fog, off Nantucket. Travelling inbound to New York on the 15th, she rammed the Nantucket Shoals lightship *No. 177* and sank her. Despite only making 3 knots at the time, *Olympic*'s sheer bulk did for the tiny light vessel. Seven of the crew were rescued from the water, but four died in the collision and three after being recovered.

It was announced that for 1935, *Olympic* would go cruising, brochures being made up and advertising taking place. In April 1935, these plans were thrown into disarray, when it was announced that *Olympic* would be laid up in Southampton and the summer season of cruises were cancelled. She was berthed behind *Mauretania* in the Western Docks in Southampton, towering over the rusty, white hull of the Cunarder. On 1 July 1935, *Mauretania* sailed from Southampton for the last time, heading for Ward's shipbreaking yard in Rosyth. Her masts were cut down to pass under the Forth Rail Bridge.

In September 1935, Sir John Jarvis MP purchased the *Olympic* for £97,500 and it was arranged that she would be sailed to Jarrow for breaking. This was despite efforts by Cunard White Star to sell her as a floating hotel. On 13 October 1935, she arrived in Jarrow for breaking. An auction sale of her fixtures and fittings was held soon after arrival and, over a period of almost two weeks, her interiors were sold. Everything from lifeboats to chairs, and from windows to paneling was auctioned. Local factories, pubs, hotels and houses were fitted out with *Olympic*'s sumptuous wood panelling, carpets and furniture. Today, it is still possible to eat in her public rooms, aboard the RCCL cruise ship *Millenium*, as well as in the White Swan Hotel, in Alnwick. However, her hull, with superstructure cut down, was towed to Inverkeithing for final breaking up in September 1937 and with that, *Olympic* had gone. She was the finest vessel in the White Star fleet and, despite the losses of her sisters, one of the most successful. Sorely missed on both sides of the Atlantic, she lived on in the memories of those who sailed in her. Of course, the auction of her fittings ensured a legacy for future generations and the author has many items from the ship, including one of her teak gymnasium windows and paneling from cabin C86, as well as items made of her brass and timbers. She was deeply loved when she was sailing and is one of the most enigmatic of passenger liners today, having a huge following among enthusiasts. Much of this love for her has come, not from her connections with *Titanic* or *Britannic*, but from her almost perfect lines and her beauty, which had not been matched before or since. It could be argued that she was the prettiest of the three sisters. In the author's opinion, the A deck enclosures did nothing for *Titanic*'s looks and the post-*Titanic* lifeboat gantries of *Britannic* spoiled the lines even more. *Olympic* retained her looks from the day she was designed to the day she was scrapped. Along with *Aquitania*, she was the classic Edwardian superliner, destined to sail alone, without a consort due to the misfortunes of her two sister ships. If only *Titanic* and *Britannic* had survived in commercial service, the history of transatlantic travel would have been so different. Instead, the White Star Line disappeared in a merger with Cunard in 1934 and the merger saw the decimation of the fleet. However, *Titanic* herself has become the most famous ship in history, the subject of numerous films, documentaries and countless books, while *Britannic* and *Olympic* tend to be overlooked, with little consideration of just how important they were in the history of ocean travel.

Left: A bookmark issued in the early 1920s, showing RMS *Olympic*.

Above, left: A photograph by Stephen Cribb of Portsmouth of a navy destroyer alongside *Olympic* in the 1920s.

Above, right: When the *Titanic* sank, White Star rebuilt *Olympic* and added a double skin. Two oil-fired boilers were also added at this time and she was fully converted post-war to oil firing.

S.16637.   R. M. S. "OLYMPIC" IN FLOATING DOCK

Opposite page, clockwise from far left: A Tourist Third Cabin brochure dating from the period of *Olympic*'s 1928–9 refit. It is full of images of not just *Olympic*, but also *Majestic* and some of the smaller Atlantic liners too.

In Ocean Dock, as it had now been renamed, the *Olympic* is berthing. It is possible to see the detail of the Cunard liner *Berengaria*'s stern.

Photographed from the Town Pier, *Olympic* is high and dry in the floating dry dock. The dry dock was acquired by the town in 1924, and officially opened by the Prince of Wales, who would become Edward VIII and then the Duke of Windsor. He had crossed on the *Olympic* in the 1920s, using a suite of cabins based around C86. The dry dock itself could lift some 60,000 tons but was made redundant upon the opening of the King George V Dry Dock, which could take 1,000-ft-long liners such as the *Queen Mary*.

Above, left: Another view of *Olympic* in dry dock, this one published by the stationers W. H. Smith, who produced many millions of cards in their Kingsway series.

Above, right: Taken from Hythe Pier, *Olympic* is outward bound from Southampton. Hythe Pier is still a ship spotter's heaven with many people viewing the huge cruise ships that visit Southampton today.

Left: A 1920s poster published by the White Star Line.

Right: This little booklet, not much bigger than a postcard, folds out to display many views of the insides of *Olympic.*

Left: Published by local Southampton photographer Rapp, *Olympic* is on her final entry into the Port of Southampton in the very early 1930s.

Below, left: Three tugs nudge *Olympic* into position to dock at berth 43.

Right: Photographed from the *Mauretania*, *Olympic* is high and dry in the floating dry dock, 1928–9.

Below: *Olympic* in dry dock, 1928–9, from *Mauretania* in the Ocean Dock.

Clockwise from left: Olympic is docked at berth 43 while the troop transport *Huntspill* has sunk at berth 38.

Montague Birrell Black's excellent cutaway of *Olympic*. This was in Haltwhistle for many years.

One of six postcards by Judges of Hastings of *Olympic* in Southampton, *c.* 1930.

A distant view of *Olympic* as photographed from a window of the South Western Hotel.

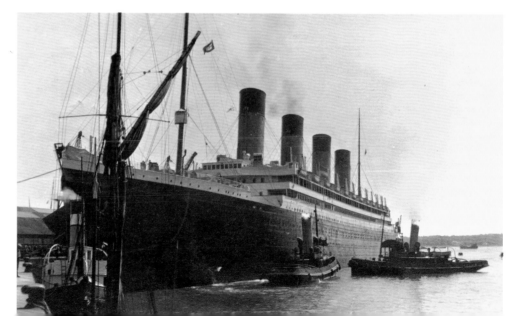

Above: Olympic and the United States Line's *Leviathan* in the Ocean Dock.

Above, right: Olympic in Ocean Dock in the late 1920s.

Right: Published after her 1928 refit, this brochure proclaims *Olympic, The Ship Magnificent.*

Below: Two snapshots of passengers aboard.

Above, left: Olympic in Southampton in the early 1930s. The tug/tender in front is the ST *Ryde*, which was once White Star's tender at Liverpool, the *Magnetic*.

Above, right: Olympic in the early 1930s, with her nested lifeboats.

Right: White Star Line's engineering staff at Southampton, aboard *Olympic*.

This page: Three views of *Olympic* in Southampton.

ENGINEERING STAFF, WHITE STAR LINE,
on January 1930 · Taken on the occasion of the retirement of Mr. J.H. Thearle

Left: Laid up at Southampton, early 1935, this view shows the towering side of *Olympic*.

Right: A series of four snapshots of *Olympic* at Jarrow, where she arrived in October 1935 for breaking.

Chapter Fifteen

FROM BUILDING TO SINKING
THE *OLYMPIC*-CLASS THROUGH THE MAIL

We all know the story; Belfast shipbuilder builds world's largest ship, shipping line proclaims it unsinkable, ship collides with iceberg and then sinks, world looks on in horror and shock as the scale of the disaster strikes.

In the past two decades, the author has been fortunate enough to come across rare and even unique postcards that tell the story of the world's most famous ship, mostly after the disaster, and sent by people unconnected with the ship, passing on gossip or just merely mentioning the disaster. Occasionally, however, one finds something out of the ordinary.

We shall begin this small journey with a short message on a card of the *Titanic* printed and published in Belfast a mere week or two before her launch, just one of many hundreds sold in the weeks leading up to the event to the residents of Belfast, proud of their upcoming new vessel. In harbour and almost ready to leave is the *Olympic*, the first of the huge White Star vessels to be completed. She would be open to the public before she set sail. The first of our cards is sent from Belfast, and shows the *Titanic* on the slipway, with a Chester-registered sailing boat in the foreground. *Titanic* herself is almost ready for launching, although the caisson wall at the end of the slipway is still in place. Graffiti adorns the wall between the Lagan and the *Titanic*'s slipway, including the names J. Kelso and E. McNairn, presumably workers from Harland & Wolff, a few of whom can be seen scrambling over the great gantry. At this time, most work on the ship would have been inside, preparing her for fitting out. Nell writes, 'We are going over the *Olympic* today it leaves Belfast Monday.' On Monday, Belfast would hold a world record, and would see the largest tonnage in any port at one time, when the two largest ships in the world would be together, docked for the first time.

Olympic would sail for Liverpool almost directly after the launch of *Titanic*, taking some of the dignitaries and press on the first voyage of the world's largest ship. Since her keel was laid in 1909, she had been a permanent fixture of the port, growing ever bigger until she was finally complete. Her sister, *Titanic*, was to be launched on the 31st and Nell again sends a card with the news. This time, she uses a card of the *Olympic* entering the Thompson Dry Dock in Belfast on 1 April 1911. The dry dock, then the largest in the world, was officially opened by the world's largest ship that day and on 31 May 1911, she sent a postcard of the event to Wellington, Somerset. She had been lucky enough to have been one of the thousands who had viewed the launch of the *Titanic* and she proudly tells Harry that 'I have been and seen the *Titanic* launched today. It went out in to the water very nicely.' By this time, she could also report on her trip over the *Olympic* saying that 'I went all over the *Olympic* on Saturday. I wish you all could have seen it. It was a grand sight.'

That afternoon, *Olympic* set sail on a journey that would last twenty-four years, through three collisions, the sinking of a U-boat and perilous journeys through mine-infested waters before she was finally sold for scrap to keep unemployed men in Northumberland in work.

Her sister, *Titanic*, was not so lucky and failed to complete a fare-paying voyage. On 10 April 1912 at noon, *Titanic* set sail for the New World, making two brief stops at Cherbourg and Queenstown. While a few passengers left at each port, many more joined the ship. In Southampton, using ticket 28228, William John Matthews, of Penwithick Stents, near St Austell, Cornwall, boarded the *Titanic* as a Second Class passenger. He

was heading for La Salle, Illinois, to meet his fiancée, and was most likely travelling with another passenger from Cornwall. Stopping at Queenstown, the *Titanic* collected many more passengers, and dropped off bags of mail written aboard the steam ship on the crossing from Southampton to the Irish port. Many of these items were kept after the sinking, poignant last memories of passengers and crew who had died, or keepsakes of lucky family members who had survived the biggest marine disaster to date. William John Matthews, or Jack to his friends, was a mere thirty years of age and he was destined never to reach Illinois, instead meeting his fate off the Grand Banks of Newfoundland. Before the ship left Queenstown, the china clay worker sent a postcard to Bill Stone, a work mate; 'Dear Bill just a line to you old boy just to let you know I am alright and well and I hope you are the same you can remember me to all well good bye from Jack.' Like most of the mail from *Titanic*, it carries an indistinct 'Queenstown, 3.45 p.m. Apr 11 12' postmark.

Little did Jack know this would be the last thing he would ever send, as on the night of 14/15 April he died and his body was never recovered. Doing some research in the 1911 Census and in the local area, it appears that Tregonissey, Bill's home, was part-way between Jack's home and the china clay works they were both employed in. It seems that Jack probably called at Bill's house every morning and they walked to work together.

As well as the ordinary people, off to a new world, the *Titanic* also carried numerous well-known passengers, from Benjamin Guggenheim to J. J. Astor and his new wife, as well as the writer W. T. Stead and the artist Frank D. Millet. Soon after the sinking, the newspapers were full of lurid stories of the sinking and from 18 April, stories from eyewitnesses and those who had travelled over the wreck site. Many bodies that were found were unidentified or unidentifiable and received burials at sea, but over 200 were recovered and laid to rest, some in mass graves in Halifax, Nova Scotia, and others in family plots. Sarah M. Millett reported the find of her cousin's body on the back of a postcard of Exmouth:

Dear Miss Haynes, Thank you very much for pretty cards. I thought that you might like this set of Exmouth, it is quite new. The disaster to the *Titanic* is too terrible to think of, and many lives lost, my American artist cousin is missing and I read in yesterday's *Daily Mail* that his body had been recovered. I expect that will be a comfort to his widow. We have still lovely sunshine, but alas also east winds which always make me bad. Kind rgards, yrs very sincerely, Sarah M. Millett.

The cousin was Frank D. Millet, who was travelling with President Taft's Aide, Major Butt, and whose body was the 259th recovered.

For weeks after the disaster, icebergs were very much in the minds of the passengers and crews of transatlantic ships, especially after a lifeboat was recovered almost a month afterwards. The next message was on a silk card of the *Lusitania*, Cunard's crack ocean liner and the second fastest ship of her day. With a Transatlantic Post Office handstamp from 25 May 1912 the card reads:

Wednesday, Dear Miss Rees, I sincerely hope that you are all quite well. Also hope your Dear Dada is no worse than when I left. I would have written from Queenstown, but I have been rather sick. Yesterday and Today I feel very well again. We are travelling rather quickly at the rate of 27 miles an hour, so you can guess how shaky we feel here. Al being well we hope to land in New York Friday morning. We are going round south today to avoid icebergs. Please give my love to your Dear Mama, Dada, your dear self and all the teachers. Emily.

Amazingly, *Titanic* was not the only sister of *Olympic* never to make a full passenger voyage. *Britannic*, the third ship of the set, had her construction halted until the results of the *Titanic* enquiries had been published. She was extensively redesigned and finally launched in February 1914. Her fitting out was delayed by the war and she was converted into a hospital ship, sailing not to New York but to Mudros in the Aegean.

This unique view, taken mere days before the launch, shows the caisson wall being removed at the end of *Britannic*'s slipway. The enigmatic message from a proud son to his father states that:

Dear father, I am making another fresh start again. Tomorrow I start work at 6 a.m. at Harland & Wolff's ship yard as electrician. Hope it will be bettering my position very soon. I have prospects of a charge hands job as soon as I have got the run of the work. Hope to let you have yours next week have not got all mine yet but will get it in a day or two. Love from all to all. I remain your loving son Fred.

Postally used on 6 September 1914, after the war had started, it is safe to assume that Fred worked on the *Britannic* until she sailed off to become a hospital ship in 1915. On 21 November 1916, *Britannic* had gone, sunk by a mine in the Aegean, and sinking in only a few minutes. The final card in our set of *Olympic*-class messages is from *Britannic*, posted immediately prior to her final departure from Southampton. Not dated, the sender was a nurse aboard and can be found on the list of survivors of the sinking. Interestingly, the card mentions the ship by name and advises of her sailing. It was obviously sent in an envelope or it would have been heavily censored.

Sunday. HMHS *Britannic* c/o GPO.
This is the boat. We came on board yesterday and are anchored off the I. of Wight at present. I expect we shall be off today. The boats we went to Malta and back on are babies compared with this. She is about the largest ship afloat and is an American liner really. Many thanks for your letter. If I am in England when you want a reference remember, I hope you will let me give you one. If I am away of course it will be different. Yours E. S. Hassall.

Britannic did indeed sail that day, for Lemnos, at 2.23 p.m. on her sixth and final voyage. A mine laid by a German submarine smashed a hole in her hull at 8.12 on the morning of 16 November and she sank in fifty-five minutes with the loss of thirty lives of the 1,066 on board. She was, in tonnage terms, the First World War's biggest shipping loss, and the largest liner ever sunk during wartime.

Of course, cards like these do not come cheap, unless you're very lucky and they all prove a point as to why you should always read the message on the back! It can be more important than the picture on the front. The cheapest of these would set

you back a couple of hundred pounds, while the one sent from the *Titanic* would be £6,000+.

S.S. "OLYMPIC" ENTERING NEW GRAVING DOCK. 1st APRIL, 1911.

This postcard has the bonus of a pretty rare view of *Olympic* entering a graving dock on the front, coupled with this superb message about the launch of the *Titanic* on the reverse.

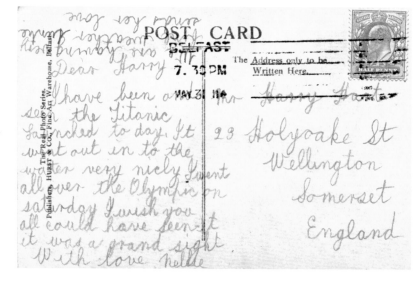

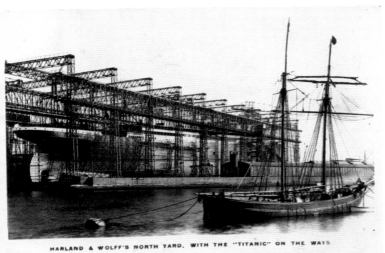

HARLAND & WOLFF'S NORTH YARD. WITH THE "TITANIC" ON THE WAYS

Left, above and below: A superb postcard of *Titanic* soon before her launch, sent in the post on the day *Olympic* was open for public inspection, prior to her departure from Belfast on 31 May 1911.

Right: the front of a postcard that has actually been aboard the *Titanic*. Cards such as this were readily and freely available on board and were used by passengers to write messages back home. This one was sent by a Second Class passenger from Cornwall who perished in the sinking. Overleaf shows the reverse of the same card.

WHITE STAR LINE.

THE LARGEST STEAMERS IN THE WORLD.

THE LARGEST STEAMERS IN THE WORLD.

"OLYMPIC" (TRIPLE-SCREW), 45,000 TONS,
AND
"TITANIC" (TRIPLE-SCREW), 45,000 TONS.

POST CARD.

For INLAND Postage (Great Britain and Ireland only), this space may be used for Correspondence.

HALFPENNY

W. H. Stone
Tregonissey
St Austell
Cornwall
England

Left: The rear of John Matthews' postcard sent to his friend Will Stone, in St Austell. The postmark is of Queenstown and is timed 3.45pm on 11 April 1912. This is the most common of all postmarks for mail sent off *Titanic*. The other postmark is a Transatlantic Post Office one.

QUEEN'S DRIVE, EXMOUTH   U188/2000

Left and right: A postcard of Exmouth sent by a cousin of Francis D. Millet in mid-April 1912. His body had just been recovered.

Published by A. Marks, Bookseller and Stationer, Exmouth.
U188/2000

Dear Miss Haynes.

Thank you very much for pretty cards. I thought that you might like this Set of Exmouth, it is quite new. The disaster to the Titanic is too terrible to think of, so many lives lost, my American Artist cousin is missing & I read in yesterdays Daily Mail, that his body had been recovered. I suppose that will be a comfort to his widow. We have still lovely Sunshine, but alas also East winds which always make me bad.

Kind regards.

Yrs. very sincerely.

Sarah. M. Millett

POST CARD. — THE ADDRESS TO BE WRITTEN HERE.

One Half-Penny Inland — One Penny Foreign

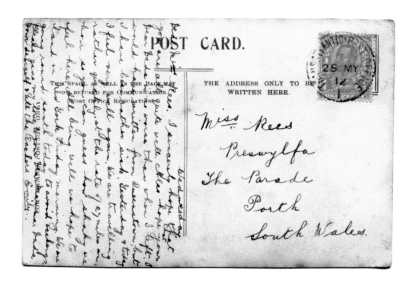

This page: These embroidered silk postcards were issued in the main by two Coventry manufacturers, W. H. Grant and Stevens. They were sold in the barber's shops aboard ship. The barber also sold many souvenirs of the vessels, from replica cap tallies to pin dishes, souvenir lifebelts, postcards, and silver and silverware items from ashtrays to buckles and badges. Postally used six weeks after the disaster, the *Lusitania* is still travelling far south to avoid icebergs, which remained a danger to navigation for a reasonable time after the *Titanic* had sunk.

Overleaf: Two postcards of *Britannic*, one at the beginning of her short and tragic life and the other at the end. The first is sent by a new employee of Harland & Wolff and the other by a nurse on her final voyage.

H.M. HOSPITAL SHIP "BRITANNIC."

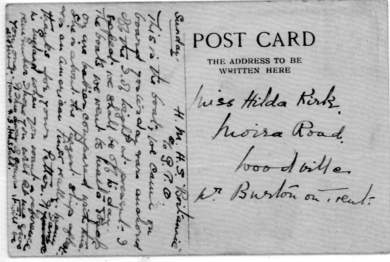